Other books by Quentin J. Schultze

The Best Family Videos: For the Discriminating Viewer (with Barbara Schultze)
Redeeming Television: How TV Changes Christians, How Christians Can Change TV
Televangelism and American Culture: The Business of Popular Religion
Dancing in the Dark: Youth, Popular Culture and the Electronic Media (coauthored)
American Evangelicals and the Mass Media (edited)
Television: Manna from Hollywood

Winning Your Kids Back from the Media

Quentin J. Schultze

INTERVARSITY PRESS
DOWNERS GROVE, ILLINOIS 60515

to Steve

InterVarsity Press® is the book-publishing division of InterVarsity Christian Fellowship®, a student movement active on campus at hundreds of universities, colleges and schools of nursing in the United States of America, and a member movement of the International Fellowship of Evangelical Students. For information about local and regional activities, write Public Relations Dept., InterVarsity Christian Fellowship, 6400 Schroeder Rd., P.O. Box 7895, Madison, WI 53707-7895.

All Scripture quotations, unless otherwise indicated, are taken from the HOLY BIBLE, NEW INTERNATIONAL VERSION®. NIV®. Copyright © 1973, 1978, 1984 by International Bible Society. Used by permission of Zondervan Publishing House. All rights reserved.

Cover photograph: Jim Whitmer

ISBN 0-8308-1398-5

Printed in the United States of America ∞

Library of Congress Cataloging-in-Publication Data

Schultze, Quentin J. (Quentin James), 1952-
    Winning your kids back from the media/Quentin J. Schultze.
        p.   cm.
    Includes bibliographical references.
    ISBN 0-8308-1398-5 (alk. paper)
    1. Mass media and children—United States.   2. Communication in the family—United States.   3. Mass media—Religious aspects—Christianity.   I. Title.
    HQ784.M3S37   1994
    302.23'083—dc20   94-18633
                                                            CIP

17	16	15	14	13	12	11	10	9	8	7	6	5	4	3	2
08	07	06	05	04	03	02	01	00	99	98	97	96	95	94	

119396

Acknowledgments

Behind every book is story. The tale behind this one is highly personal, as the reader will soon see.

My wife, Barb, is an enormously gifted person who truly knows how to love. I thank God for creating her that way, and for sharing her with me in the task of parenting.

Steve and Beth are kindhearted children who echo their mother's gift of loving others. As my firstborn, Steve helped to train his dad in the wise ways of charitable fathering.

InterVarsity Press was so wonderful to work with on an earlier book, *Redeeming Television,* that I was delighted to sit in their publishing courts once again. IVP is loaded with people of faith, integrity and good cheer. I thank God for all of them, especially laconic Rodney Clapp, the only editor I know who approaches a manuscript like a country songwriter strumming on the guitar—with passion, a deft hand and melodic zeal.

Thanks, too, to Lois Curley. Her experience in publishing takes the burden of finding the right press off my back and lets me concentrate on writing. It also gives me more time for parenting in this crazy media world.

Through it all there is inexplicable grace.

Introduction

Not long ago I visited an outstanding bookstore with a large section on parenting. Beginning with the first book in the section, I took each one off the shelf to see what it said about family communication, as well as about the newer media technologies such as cable TV, VCRs, video games and computers.

I was surprised at how few parenting books even *mentioned* the new media technologies. More amazing still, many of them had nothing significant to say about family communication! I concluded that authors of books on parenting apparently assume that people know how to communicate. I believe that they are wrong.

At the same time, I was surprised to find a wealth of magazines on parenting, including such titles as *Child, Parenting, Family Life* and *Family Fun.* It seemed to me, as I browsed these publications, that they were written for a new generation of parents who never learned parenting from their own parents. They held up parent-child interaction like a precious commodity and offered all kinds of ways of spending leisure time together. Among the activities that parents and children can share, of course, are media.

We live in a high-tech world with more communication gadgets than Alexander Graham Bell and Jules Verne probably could have imagined. The other day my teenage son connected his computer in Michigan with a computer in California via another computer in Minnesota. Then he transmitted video images over two thousand miles into the privacy of our home. During the Gulf War in 1992 he and I watched live coverage of the conflict—the first war shown partly live by the magic of satellites and cable. While vacationing in the Great Smoky Mountains, my daughter listened privately on headphones to audiotapes produced by a Christian organization in Colorado.

Today's families live in a new electronic global city that is rapidly engulfing the home. Over the next few years parents will face a barrage of new technologies such as electronic mail, digital recording and fiber optics. The day before I wrote this introduction, *Time* magazine announced that it will soon make the periodical available on one of the major computer information services. Families will be able to read the magazine on their home computers before it hits the newsstands and arrives in mailboxes. It will not be long before many periodicals and even entire libraries are accessible via computers. Also, five-hundred-channel cable TV systems are just around the corner.

This is a different world from the one I grew up in. We baby boomers thought it was really "neat" to tune in a top-40 radio station on our new Sears transistor radios, which we hid under our pillows, listening long into the night to groups like the Four Seasons and artists like Elvis Presley and Buddy Holly. My parents worried primarily about who their kids "hung out with" at school and around the neighborhood. Only the movies caused them to wonder about potentially bad media influences, but back then kids had to go *out* to the movies; the movies couldn't come *into* the home. The family seemed to be protected from the more wicked media.

Since then the media world has changed radically. Teen-oriented radio stations popped up all over the FM dial, cable TV grew with offerings like HBO, Comedy Central and MTV, satellites revived national radio shows such as Rush Limbaugh's, cellular auto and pocket phones spread across the country, and VCRs became virtually a necessity for many families. Now the computer is linking homes and businesses around the world. Recently I saw a news report that pornography is being "transported" via computer networks from Europe to the United States and presumably the rest of the world.

This book looks at family life in the electronic age. I show how parents can take advantage of the new high-tech world of communications to enhance family life. But I also warn families caught up in the electronic revolution: high-tech media are threatening low-tech family communication. As many family members are happily spending more time with their electronic media, they're abandoning communication with each other. Today many North American families are media-rich and communication-poor. Too much leisure time is dedicated to selfish media consumption, and far too little to precious family conversation, storytelling and listening. It's time we won our children back from the media.

I don't believe families can survive the onslaught of high-tech communications without a corresponding commitment to building deep, rewarding relationships with one another and with close friends. As I argue in chapter two, the North American family is particularly vulnerable to high-tech saturation. Middle- and upper-middle-class families are so busy with the "business" of media leisure that the family is becoming a mere economic unit instead of a group of loving individuals who share values and beliefs and, most important of all, who selflessly serve each other.

All media are tools for building "commonness" among people. This commonness is the basis of relationship. Changes in communication affect family relationships, and all changes in family relationships will influence how families use high- and low-tech media. Like fish in water, however, we don't see many of these connections between family life and media. We complain about offensive media content because it's so obvious, but we miss more subtle and pervasive changes.

When my wife and I were first married, we agreed to put our small TV set in a living-room closet. Either of us could watch television whenever we wanted, but the inconvenience of taking the set out of the closet and setting it up on a table was enough to discourage idle viewing. We now realize that was one of the smartest things we did during our early years together, because it fostered the simple joy of spending time together in neighborhood walks, backyard gardening and home repairs. We conversed at great length during these activities, getting to know each other as special individuals with particular gifts and needs.

By the time our first child was born, we knew much about our mutual interests and incompatibilities. From then on, we built our shared relationship while simultaneously nurturing each other's individual gifts. It was not always easy. Just as communication can be the cement of rewarding relationships, it can be the wrecking ball. Family-building is a lifelong process of loving communication.

Parents need to teach their children to be faithful stewards of both low- and high-tech communication. In biblical terms, parents' responsibility includes learning with their offspring how to communicate with patience, love and joy. We need to help more families become media stewards who nurture God-pleasing relationships. These relationships, in turn, are a witness to the rest of the world of the lordship of Christ. All media are gifts from God. They should be used to his glory.

Four basic principles guide this book:

Discernment. Not all media messages are good for family members, and we need to learn to discern among high-tech (media) and low-tech (family) messages.

Moderation. Too much or too little media communication is not good for family life; the new media are worthwhile if used in moderation.

Balance. Families should balance high- and low-tech communication with nonmedia family time.

Integration. Media should be integrated into family life through discussion and family use, rather than be used only privately by individual members.

As these four principles suggest, media use is an important part of family life. Chapter three offers many practical suggestions for building family life in a media world without going cold turkey. The following chapter goes even a step further, providing ideas for parents who want to turn the problem of media use into an opportunity for building spiritual discernment in a media age.

The next two chapters, five and six, look at the parenting of young children and teens in the electronic world. There is so much misinformation about this topic in the popular media, especially TV and newspapers, that I decided to present a basic overview of the subject with many examples. I ask parents to suspend their biases before reading those chapters. It would be great if parents and children read the appropriate chapter together and then openly discussed it.

Some of the highly critical, knee-jerk responses to youth media have made it difficult for families to discuss the topic. Many children know that their parents are naively misinformed about the media. This, too, is one of the results of an electronic world, where children are sometimes more media-savvy, though not more discerning, than their parents. Children need essentially three things to be adequately prepared for their own adult responsibilities in a media world: (1) access to media technologies, (2) values for using the technologies and (3) adult role models and mentors, especially parents.

It's no longer realistic to think of raising children in a media vacuum. Kids today are tuned in and turned on to the media more than any previous generation. These media transport our children out of the home and take them on "rides" to other cultures. Sometimes they journey back in time to the peaceful if unrealistic world of the Beaver or the rural world of Mayberry. Other times our children navigate the treacherous cultures of MTV, teen flicks, video games and the coming world of "virtual reality."

Unless we trash all media and move our families to an undeveloped country, there will be no entirely safe haven from the media world. Instead of a castle or a haven, the home is becoming the *center* of the media world, the place where all media converge for fun and profit. During the last two centuries, North America has been transformed from a place of villages to cities, to metropolises, to the new electronic "supercity" connecting individual homes to the growing network of worldwide communication. In this new media world it makes no difference if a family lives on a farm or in an urban condo. All face the same media threats and have the same media opportunities.

The coming media world won't be universally affordable, but it will reach its tentacles into nearly every home, business and vehicle—if not every pocket and purse. As the new communications technologies become smaller and cheaper, and as children see their friends using the new media, parents will join the communications revolution. Otherwise parents will find themselves living in a very different world from the one their offspring inhabit.

Suddenly we've reached an era in which youth seem to be more proficient media users than their parents. Adults are increasingly followers, not leaders, in the communications revolution. Anthropologist Margaret Mead suggested in *Culture and Commitment* that North America might be the first cultural experiment where "tradition" flows backwards. In other words, we might reach a point where youth transmit culture to parents, rather than the elders of society passing wisdom on to the children. One wonders, if there is any validity to Mead's claim, whether a society could survive without historical memory, parental authority and especially religious tradition. This becomes a real threat as the media bombard youth with new messages—the latest products, the hottest rock groups, the newest fashions, the current media idols. Unless parents help to slow down this cultural barrage, and replace much of it with loving authority built on spiritual wisdom, modern culture could implode under the pressure of its own selfish search for novelty.

In any case, one thing is clear: the media compete directly with parents, pastors and teachers for the job of raising children. Each of these groups of traditional authority figures is increasingly distraught over the apparent power of the media to shape youth's values and beliefs. Unless parents become wise about the opportunities as well as the liabilities of media use, parenting will be transferred to communications moguls, media conglomerates and media idols. It's time to win back our children without trashing the wonderful gifts the new media can bring.

1
Mission Possible

Communicating
for Fun and Family

Our young daughter announced proudly at the dinner table that she had decided what to be when she grew up—an archaeologist. My wife and I were stunned. Did she even know what an archaeologist was? A doctor or teacher we could understand, but not an archaeologist.

So I prodded a bit: "Do you know what archaeologists do?"

"Yes," she replied tenaciously, as if expecting me to talk her out of it.

"Well," I asked, "why do *you* want to be an archaeologist?"

Without hesitating she gave an answer that I will never forget: "Because I can find things in my room."

She had us cold. Her logic was impressive. After all, looking for anything in her room was like searching for a precious bone fragment in a massive archaeological dig. She had been saved on more than one occasion by the only remaining explanation for missing objects: "The dog must have taken it." We all knew that *was* possible: fox terriers are archaeologists in reverse. They bury cultural artifacts, especially socks.

My daughter's vocational announcement reflects in a nutshell what parenting and family life are all about: communication. Children are trying to discover who they are, how they should act and what they will be. Parents are teachers and role models, explicitly and implicitly passing along to their children a way of life. All of this happens—for good and bad—through the glorious gift of communication.

The First Parents

I've often wondered what it was like for Adam to stand before the face of God and name the creatures. Did he just blurt out sounds for every critter? Or did he give the project a bit of thought, perhaps relating names to animal sounds or other features?

Once, while teaching a course on television criticism, I asked the students to rename the characters on their favorite soap operas. The catch was that the names had to be *animal* names. In a strange reversal of Adam's original role, the students were to imagine what types of animals were like soap stars.

After a few false starts, the class caught on to the assignment. Bedlam ensued. We had sly foxes, silly monkeys, "ready" rabbits and stubborn jackasses. By the end of the class the students had an entirely different image of soaps as a rather savage kingdom that turns human beings into animals.

When Adam and Eve began naming the creatures, they were not just exercising the gift of linguistic freedom. They began a job that we inherited, the task of using communication to decide who we are and how we should live. Biblically speaking, the "name" of something is a symbol for its true meaning. The Bible is filled with such meaningful names, from Adam (roughly "man" or "humankind") to Ishmael ("God hears") to Bethany ("House of Misery"—our daughter's name, and an appropriate one for the offspring of a college professor who *thinks* he can keep things running around the house). In the New Testament, the apostle Paul was first named Saul, until his dramatic conversion changed his identity before God and in the eyes of the nascent church.

Parenting is mostly communication. Adults use verbal and nonverbal communication to create an *identity* for themselves and their offspring. In the best possible world, parents are supported in this task by other social institutions, such as schools and churches. But the real world is not nearly so simple and supportive. Conflicting messages abound, and most children grow up in a confusing world of competing "names" for who they are. Peers may tell them one thing ("You are an athletic star"), teachers another ("You are an undependable student"), pastors yet another ("You are a sinner" or "You are a child of God") and so on.

I will never forget the day in high-school Spanish class when my teacher shook her head, clicked her tongue and said to me in front of the other students, "You're lazy!" That name hurt, even if it was a little true. The fact was that my problems at home made it hard to concentrate on schoolwork. I was more "troubled" than lazy, but she didn't know any better.

This communication breakdown echoes the Fall of our first parents, who arrogantly ate the forbidden fruit. Instead of gaining true knowledge of who they were, Adam and Eve became guilty and embarrassed sinners. They hid from God and from each other, as if by not communicating they could solve their problem. Then, to make matters even worse, they lied to themselves and to God about their sinful deeds in the Garden of Eden.

All of us bring this sinfulness into our parenting. We fail to communicate when we should, thereby turning the task of parenting over to others. We mistakenly blame others, including spouses and children, for our own inadequacies or misdeeds. Sometimes we even get on a high horse, blasting the government or schools for causing our nation's children to stumble, when often the real villain is ourselves. We simply fail to use the gift of communication to create a stable, loving identity for our family. Instead, we selfishly or thoughtlessly squander this precious gift.

You Are What You Communicate

When I was growing up in Illinois during the 1960s and 1970s, there was a popular expression among health-food advocates: "You are what you eat." It was an attractive shibboleth in those days, almost like a secret proverb among the nutritionally wise who believed that diet dictated a person's physical, emotional and even spiritual health.

A far more biblical saying might be "You are what you communicate." Although we're certainly born with particular personality traits and physical characteristics, our values and beliefs are formed largely by the people and media in our lives. Communication is the crucial process through which we learn a "culture" or way of life. Communication shapes our self-image, which in turn influences others around us, including our children.

In the powerful film *Not Without My Daughter,* Sally Field plays an upper-middle-class Michigan resident married to an Iranian doctor. When Field, her husband and her young daughter travel to Iran after the fall of the Shah, presumably to visit her husband's family, Field suddenly finds herself trapped in a culture that is alien to her. She must learn the local language and customs if she is ever to live in harmony with her husband and his Islamic extended family.

The film is extremely moving, and even frightening, because it dramatizes how precious communication is for all of us who value the freedom to choose our own way of life. Field becomes an unsuspecting victim of a group of seemingly well-intentioned Muslims who seek to control virtually all communication with her in the name of truth and the revolution. The telephone is disconnected, her money for transportation is taken away, and her interaction with any non-Iranian citizens is virtually eliminated. Under Iranian law, her daughter belongs only to her husband. Field's character is apparently left with two unacceptable alternatives: either to become an Iranian Muslim and live in harmony with her husband's family or to lapse into an isolated, depressing existence cut off from virtually all meaningful relationships. For the sake of her daughter and Iranian-born son, she instead boldly risks her life to escape the country and return to America, where she can communicate freely and raise her children in the values and beliefs she cherishes.

Field's basic dilemma in the film is an exaggerated version of the responsibility faced by all parents. The choices we make about who we and our children communicate with will significantly shape the values and beliefs our families share. It's not possible to put our children's heads in the sand by prohibiting our offspring from communicating with anyone. As children grow up and eventually mature, their circles of friends and patterns of media use rapidly expand, like the self-inflicted imposition of a "foreign" culture on their minds and hearts. What they watch, hear and read will contribute to their identity.

One of the greatest myths of modern society is that the media are essentially in the entertainment or information business. Mass media, as vehicles of communication, are more fundamentally in the *identity* business. They create and/or reflect the basic values and beliefs of the people who use them. It's not always easy to determine which comes first, the media's views of reality or our own views. But make no mistake about it, the media are major purveyors of identity in our world.

Usually by the high-school years, and certainly during college, young people's diet of communication over the previous two decades has had an enormous influence on their lives. Depending significantly on the loving role of their parents as personal communicators, these image-bearers of God may become loyal and joyful members of God's community.

Ironically, the major dilemma today for most parents is how to cope positively with the abundance of mass communicators who want a chance to "name" others' children. There is neither one North American culture nor one community, but an increasingly worldwide supermarket of media products and professional communicators. And as we shall see in chapter four, the revolution in high-tech communications will make the situation even more complex. The solution is not only to make wise judgments about which high-tech communicators we will invite into our families, but also to revive in our homes and churches the low-tech arts of conversation, listening and storytelling. These basic human abilities are essential tools for rebuilding the community known as "family."

Family as Community

By the grace of God, communication can be the cement for strong, enduring family relationships. The Latin root for the word *communication* means literally "to make common." It's the same basic root for the words *community* and *communion.* The joy of family communication is creating a "common" family life that pleases God, fulfills our basic needs for identity and intimacy (close emotional relationship), and equips children eventually to become loving parents themselves. Communication thus enables us to fellowship with each other and with God.

Paul Benware, professor of Bible and theology at Moody Bible Institute, nicely describes this "fellowship" as "the idea of relationship, partnership, and communion. It is the sharing of common life with mutual concerns, interests, and other resources. Fellowship with one another means sharing the burdens and blessings of the Christian life." Does this describe your family?

I know firsthand the difficulty of finding one's way in life without the common values and beliefs that make a family a community. For one thing, I was the last-born of three sons, and my two older brothers were practically gone by the time I reached adolescence. As a child, I shared little of my life with them. Only now, decades later, am I building community with them across thousands of miles. Thank God for telephones, airplanes and even automobiles that enable us to re-create family life over geographic barriers!

More important, by the time I was born my parents were already headed toward divorce. I was shuttled back and forth between them, and I grew up experiencing their differences, not their shared lives. The community was divided, and there seemed to be no hope for getting it back together.

I recall vividly being on my knees as a young child, pleading tearfully with God to restore my familial community. Twenty years later, God did just that, but in a far greater way than I ever could have imagined as a hurting child. God gave me a spouse and two wonderful children. This is the family I prayed for. The curse was broken by grace: no longer will the children's teeth be "set on edge" just because "the fathers have eaten sour grapes" (Jeremiah 31:29; Hebrews 8:8-12).

Although my parents never reunited, eventually I experienced additional grace through the joy of communication with my aged mother. Since the time I first dated, my mother would not have anything to do with women in my life. In fact, she refused to come to my wedding, one of the most meaningful events of my life. But not long before she died, I happened to ask Mother about her childhood in Chicago, especially during the Great Depression. My question was merely an attempt to make conversation about matters that didn't divide us, but her answer forever changed my understanding of her burdens.

She told me a heart-wrenching story of the hardship faced by her large family. Much of it involved predictable Depression-era situations and events. But as her personal narrative flowed, so did the tears of pain and eventually anger. Her parents had taken in two young women and treated them like daughters. They became the "model" girls of the family, and my mother was deeply hurt by her parents' repeated admonitions to her, "Why can't you be like your sisters?" Those troubling years greatly shaped my mother's character and, years later, made her deeply suspicious of any women who might enter her own family.

When I retold this story to my older brothers, they were equally astonished. How was it that none of us had ever asked Mother the right questions? How could we have so easily let divisions separate the family, without ever looking for the personal stories behind those divisions? Like Adam and Eve, we had been trying to forget the past, perhaps hiding out of our own hurt and shame.

Apart from our relationship to Christ, who sees everything in our heart, families offer the best opportunities for deeply rewarding communication. Through the marvelous gift of communication we come to know each other and to love each other. As we "commune," we share our lives and build community. Communication is often the wrecking ball that destroys relationships, but it can also be a blessed means of expressing our love and building each other up.

Communication and Love

Communication is far more wonderful than just a tool for families to create community. It also enables us to "commune" deeply with another person, to see and respect each other as distinctive creatures, what Fred Rogers calls our "special" self, and to serve one another's specific needs. In short, communication makes it possible for us to give ourselves lovingly to others.

It is impossible for us to love people whom we don't know. This is as true for our relationships with family members as it is for our "communion" with Christ. By giving us the gift of communication, God made it possible for us to break out of our loneliness and to fellowship with each other and with him. Animals cannot do this; their communication is relatively primitive and highly instinctual. They cannot love, although they can be affectionate and lovable.

By communicating with their children, parents can come to know each daughter, each son, as a special person endowed with particular gifts and faced with individual needs. The three most important communication techniques for building this type of loving relationship are storytelling, listening and empathizing.

Storytelling

Family *storytelling* is sharing our real-life experiences with each other. It includes telling others what happened and how we felt about it.

Stories of this type enable an entire family to share one member's life.

Every evening at dinner we go around the table, telling each other the stories of our day. Some are humorous, others sad or even maddening, but each story brings us closer together as a family.

As in the case of my mother's Depression-era story, personal narratives can be quite revealing. This is why so much counseling is based on personal storytelling. My wife and I have learned an enormous amount about our children from the stories they tell about school, play, friends, summer camp and the like. Similarly, they've learned much about us from our parental storytelling.

Several years ago my preteen son asked me what it is like to be a teenager. It was a great question, and I could have answered with professional insight: "Teenagers experience growing generational segregation, identity and intimacy crises, and, of course, hormonal changes resulting in . . ." He would have rolled his eyes and called up a friend for some real answers. So I did something entirely different: I told him stories of my own teenage years.

We began the excursion into my past by renting and viewing together the film *American Graffiti.* I selected that film partly because it's set in the period when I was growing up and partly because it captures the adolescent innocence that's so often missing in today's teen flicks. Most of the movie takes place at a fast-food drive-in, similar to the one that was built in my own hometown. And the characters, although somewhat stereotypical, reflect the basic divisions among high-school youth in the 1960s.

After the filmic look at teenage life, we made a trip to my boyhood home, where I narrated on location some of my early years. When I first asked my son if he would like to visit my old stomping grounds, I was not expecting such an enthusiastic response. In fact, my daughter and wife immediately expressed interest as well, so we turned the trip into a family event. Of course, much of my story was laced with parental observations about my own youth. As long as the lessons were part of the personal narrative, the children loved them. Yet if I had made some of the same points abstractly, without the story, my kids would probably not have been nearly as interested and open.

Parental storytelling is a powerful form of instruction because it carries the weight of experience and conveys the joy of community. Jean Shepherd, one of my favorite contemporary American novelists, believes that even fictionalized first-person accounts of growing up can be a considerable source of comfort to readers who recognize that they went through similar trials and tribulations as well as comparable triumphs. His wacky video movie *Olie Hopnoodle's Haven of Bliss* wonderfully captures old-fashioned auto vacations to "the lake." It will rekindle all kinds of vacation memories to tell your children, as it did for my wife. For parents, personal narratives are like parables of family life that implicitly instruct the kids while reminding the parents of lessons they learned—or should have learned.

Listening

Listening is also important for building loving relationships in families. Far too many parents invest time in speaking to their children but very little time in listening to them. Listening is admittedly much harder. I believe that the Fall makes most of us rather selfish communicators, jumping at the chance to insert our two cents' worth even if we don't understand the other person. On buses and planes I've even heard "conversations" in which both of the parties were talking at the same time. This might be speech, but it certainly isn't communication.

Listening is primarily the receiving end of storytelling. It is trying to reconstruct in our own minds the events and feelings experienced by someone else. When a child has a problem, we need to listen to the story that gave rise to the problem before we offer a solution.

Our family's move to a new house taught me the profound value of listening. My wife and I were delighted with the benefits of the move for our children: their own play area in the house, a nearby swimming pool, more privacy for our adolescent son, greater play possibilities with a larger backyard, and more privacy for Dad when he was writing, so the kids wouldn't have to be so quiet during summer days. When the children continued to complain about the move up to a year after we made it, we were emotionally demolished. Partly out of a lack of alternatives, we began listening to the kids rather than trying to sell them on the already-completed move.

What we heard shocked our foolish hearts: the loss of neighborhood friends, the loss of the only house they had ever lived in, even the fear of losing all of the memories of events that occurred in the old house—birthday parties, the time the lights went out during a tornado warning, special meals and visits of friends and relatives. We listened to all of it. And then we grieved with the children, because they were right about the losses. No move is entirely a gain, except in the colored vision of optimistic parents. But after the grieving was over, the new place looked much better to all of us.

In my experience, wives seem much better at listening than husbands. My wife regularly alerts me to family problems or joys that I somehow missed. Husbands, listen to your wives. Wives, speak the truth in love to your deaf husbands.

Empathy

Finally, loving family relationships require empathy. When we listen, we have to put ourselves in the shoes of storytellers. And when we tell our own tales, we must be careful to empathize with the listeners.

Psychologist James Dobson once remarked in an interview, "The key to raising healthy, responsible children is to be able to get behind the eyes of the child and see what he sees, think what he thinks and feel what he feels. If you know how to do that, then you know how to respond appropriately for him." This is true wisdom.

The deepest and most rewarding relationships in a family are built upon empathy. Christ experienced a human death on our behalf. His love for us was remarkably empathic. Although we are unable to empathize to the unfathomable degree of Christ, our human nature permits far more empathy than most of us will ever experience. Like Adam and Eve, we would rather hide or blame than truly empathize.

My wife, a part-time home-health nurse, has found that real patient care is simply not possible without considerable empathy. She can't determine all of a patient's needs with purely physical assessment or textbook medical orthodoxy. She has found that every patient's story is more or less different from all others, including those who have the same formal medical diagnosis. As a result, she adjusts her care for each patient as she better understands their particular emotional, physical and spiritual needs.

So it is with parenting. A former colleague of mine, himself a father of nine children, used to tell me that God gives children to parents in order to discipline the parents. I've since concluded that he was half right. God also gives parents to children in order to discipline the children. The truth is that you have to have both kinds of discipline for a truly gratifying family life. In my judgment, parental empathy for children may be the most lacking form of communicative discipline in our modern workaday world.

The clue to successful empathizing is to suspend judgment until the story is fully told. As Mother Teresa once said, "If you judge people, you have no time to love them." Love waits on judgment until the facts are in and the person is known. Quick, thoughtless responses to loved ones are signs of a lack of selfless empathy and symptoms of an overly critical spirit.

If a story sounds too implausible to be true, or if the narrative just doesn't make sense, it's the responsibility of the listener to ask questions. The best queries are relatively open-ended: "What happened next?" "Why did you do that?" "How did you feel?" These kinds of questions are invitations to the storyteller to continue, but they are also implicit affirmations of the inherent value of the storyteller. Just by asking questions instead of launching into evaluation or judgment, we say to the storyteller, "I care about you and your experiences."

Communicating by Example

Perhaps the most sobering aspect of parenting is the fact that parents communicate as much *implicitly*, by what they do, as by explicitly teaching their children. All of our verbal and nonverbal actions "speak" to others, especially to those who live with us. Our loved ones catch us off guard, when our façades are thin and our defenses are low. More than those with whom we work and worship, our families see the real person behind the public image. All of our actions tell these loved ones who we are. They all communicate our underlying values and beliefs, not just what we *say* we value and believe.

Once we realize this fundamental fact of our createdness, we must admit that parenting is never a part-time job. Whenever we are with our loved ones, even when they hear indirectly about us from others, we are parenting. As I suggested previously, parenting is primarily communication. Now you see that communication is not merely what we say or do when we're acting officially as parents, but communication is the entire "statement" we make about ourselves in the course of carrying out our duties as well as enjoying ourselves in this world.

All of our actions tell others who we are.

Process over Product

Parenting is sometimes a struggle, but it is also a wonderful opportunity to use our God-given gifts of communication to enrich family life and prepare children for lives of grateful service to God. In my experience, too many economically comfortable parents see parenting as labor instead of as an adventure worth enjoying and celebrating. Parenting is indeed a lot of work, and it is certainly more complicated in a media world, but it is not just demanding labor. We can use communication to build deep and rewarding closeness, to establish God-pleasing identities and to serve those whom we love. The results will never be perfect, but the loving process can cover a multitude of sins (1 Peter 4:8).

My wife manages to find enjoyment in ordinary, even menial tasks by sharing them with family. She learned while growing up how to transform a routine family car trip into a journey of games, wordplay and reminiscences. The kids like to shop with her because it's fun, even if nothing is purchased; it's the looking and talking. Somehow she even manages to turn yardwork into communication, drawing the kids into raking leaves and diving into the piles.

If we focus too much on the "product" of parenting, we'll likely lose the joy of the process. My wife and I have learned this the hard way, because we, too, want our children to succeed in life. We've pushed sometimes for good school grades and for more practice hours on their musical instruments. I've even bugged my teenage son, a budding actor, about getting his résumé ready. All of this speaks volumes about the values of yuppie parents caught on the slopes of upward mobility. It is one thing to want the best for our children, and quite another thing to create a loving atmosphere in which parents and children alike can honestly seek God's will for their lives with encouragement and support.

In one of his better-known songs, the balladeer Harry Chapin once wrote, "It's got to be the going, not the gettin' there." The "going" of family communication and parenting in a media world has got to be good.

If you would like a more enriching and God-pleasing family life, join me on an excursion into parental communication. There are many rewards—and not just in heaven or when the children finally become well-adjusted, responsible adults. The "going" in parenting is often fun, enjoyable and sometimes even heartwarming for all members of the family.

What would you do in *this* real scenario? During breakfast with my two young children, I sink into the usual professorial stupor while my mind races to the heady lectures I have to deliver during the day. In the process, with my daughter watching, I stand up, shuffle over to the nearby garbage can, pop the lid lever with my foot and begin unzipping my pants to relieve my bladder.

Daughter Beth, enormously puzzled, asks the only reasonable question: "Dad, what are you doing?"

With that the intellectual spell is broken, and I return to an embarrassing reality. She has told this story of her absent-minded professor-dad over and over again. Every time it reminds her that even Dad is like a little kid sometimes. Indeed we dads are—and so are moms. Thank God!

The Treasure of Time

Frequently when a loved one dies the grieving family members wish that they had had even a few more hours or one extra day with the deceased. The grievers sadly rehearse all the things they wish they had said or done and sometimes even recall the harsh words or misdeeds that hurt the deceased. They long for more time; they wish they had honored the *process* of being together.

I was blessed when my daughter announced at the dining table her archaeological future, when my son and I viewed *American Graffiti* together and even when my mother revealed her private wounds of sibling jealousy. Through all of these experiences I not only communed with my family but also experienced some of the joy of childhood that I had been denied as a child. Whatever the final product of these moments of family communication, they were all part of that process of grace, the shalom of parenting.

Although these essentials of parental communication remain the same today as always, the context of family life has changed radically in the media world. We have to manage storytelling, listening and empathy in a society saturated with conflicting messages about who we are and what we should value in life. All of this takes time, perhaps the most squandered resource in a media world.

2
Family Matters

How We Got Here

My family rarely goes camping, partly because of my allergies and my wife's sensitivities to poisonous plants. But a few years ago we spent an evening at a state park with friends who regularly vacation in tents. I wasn't sure what to expect, other than mosquitoes and smoke. I was the curious anthropologist studying these "primitive" people.

Sitting on logs and taking in the sights and sounds of modern camping, I came to a startling conclusion: most of the campers were technological missionaries, not urban exiles. They brought along practically every communications technology imaginable. As dusk approached, you could see families gathered around the bluish glow of portable television sets, as if around a fire. Everywhere I walked in the park, I could hear portable CD and tape players as well as radios. Some of them were high-fidelity stereo systems installed in vans and campers. A few cellular phone antennas popped up here and there. There were apparently VCRs in RVs, because the video-rental shop down the road from the campground was doing a brisk business. I had the strange sense that some campers were actually showing off their technological gadgets: the sounds were too loud for private enjoyment, and a good deal of media use was occurring in the open. Was this "technological witnessing"?

Since that excursion into the state park, I've concluded that modern camping symbolizes the state of parenting in a media world. From World War II to the present, leisure time has been increasingly gobbled up by mass media. High-tech media have steadily eclipsed low-tech communication. For all of the growth in personal and family income, producing greater leisure dollars, we have not improved family relationships, increased marital harmony or raised more godly children. In fact, the family is slowly being transformed into an economic unit, gathered around the media camp, pretending to be bonded together by love and commitment.

Of course, media are not the only culprits. Changes in work habits, greater mobility and other technological developments are also important factors. In lectures I have often joked with audiences that the invention of the automatic dishwasher was a wicked plot to destroy family communication. Much family discussion used to take place around the kitchen sink after meals. Similarly, the automobile made it easy for older teens to escape the house and meet privately with peers. A lot of teens were "educated" at drive-in theaters and fast-food restaurants during the 1950s and 1960s, much as they are today at shopping malls.

Media technologies greatly restructured family communication patterns. Naive and sometimes selfish parents loaded their own leisure time with media consumption and often encouraged children to do the same. The result is a land of pseudofamilies bonded together primarily by economic necessities instead of by love and service. They know who's responsible for bringing home the paycheck, taking out the garbage, driving the kids to school, paying the bills, cooking meals and cleaning house. All of these "essentials" are covered, but it's not clear whose responsibility it is to foster family "communication." As long as individual family members can escape to their own media "campgrounds," life goes on until the income stops or unfulfilled needs are expressed.

Work and Time

In her revealing book *The Overworked American,* Juliet B. Schor states that half the population says it has too little time for family. Feeling frazzled and frenzied, Americans say that they don't have enough time to give to each other, including to close family and friends. "Today," she says, "many families haven't got the time to care." One of the major culprits, she suggests, is overwork.

Some of her research seems to support this conclusion. She and her economist-colleague Laura Leete-Guy conclude that between 1969 and 1989 the average annual time spent on the job by Americans rose by eighty-six hours. Meanwhile, time for vacations, personal days, sick leave and holidays declined about 15 percent. According to these data, employed Americans now work the equivalent of about an extra month each year.

Other studies, using different methods of measuring work time, conclude that it has actually decreased. John P. Robinson, head of the Americans' Use of Time Project, found that work time has dropped over the last twenty years. More people are working, but they are working on average fewer hours each week. White-collar professionals, for instance, may take more time off during the workday to run errands or to take children to the doctor. Similarly, people who work out of their home usually have more flexibility in juggling work with personal activities.

In spite of these disagreements over the actual amount of time Americans work, there is nearly unanimous agreement that we *feel* as if we have less time for nonwork activities. Even our off-work hours seem frenzied, overscheduled and underenjoyed. Robinson found that 32 percent of Americans "almost always" feel "rushed." According to a *New York Times* poll, 85 percent of working mothers and 72 percent of working fathers said they were torn between the demands of work and the desire to spend more time with their families. This may be why two-thirds of Americans said in a 1992 survey that they would give up some income in exchange for more time for themselves and to be with their families. In another poll, half of all Americans said they would give up a day's pay every week for an additional day off.

Feeling ourselves caught in this kind of frenzy, my family decided that the extra income generated by two full-time incomes wasn't worth the extra stress and lost family time. My wife works only part-time, reserving two or three days per week for the family. Similarly, I have had to say no to many requests to speak or to write articles.

In the industrialized West we have created overscheduled family lives that produce the stress of work even when we're not actually working. Work is our *attitude*, not just our means of employment or professional vocation. We work not only "on the job" but also in the yard, around the house, at the cottage and in the kitchen. We "work" at parenting, at shopping and even at sports, scheduling these activities often as if they were part of an itinerary for personal or family success. The sheer joy of the activities, their spontaneous pleasure, is not enough. We want to succeed at leisure, and before long leisure becomes work. So we work harder to make more money, supposedly to enjoy such "leisure."

What's Happened to Leisure?

Interestingly enough, even though most of us feel as if we don't have leisure time, we actually have plenty of it. Robinson discovered that individuals have roughly forty hours weekly of "free time"—more than people had twenty years ago. In spite of all of the two-wage-earner families, which are now a national norm, there may even be greater average leisure time than there was among earlier generations.

The *apparent* disappearance of leisure results partly from a few changes in parental responsibility. One is the growing number of single-parent families. Almost one-third of families with children are single-parent, and 90 percent of them are headed by women. There are fewer *Leave It to Beaver* families, where the mother stays home to take care of domestic chores that might otherwise reduce leisure time. Also, about one-quarter of Americans live alone, up from 8 percent fifty years ago. Finally, about 10 percent of couples between the ages of forty and sixty have one or more parents still living, and over half of these couples have *two* living parents. Undoubtedly people in all of these situations feel as if they have less free time because of their increased responsibilities outside the workplace.

All of these studies and statistics can be deceptive without one crucial point: Regardless of whether actual leisure time has increased or decreased, what leisure time there is has become primarily a time for individual media consumption. In North America, mass media use has eclipsed most family activities. The evidence for this is both amazing and depressing.

Boobis Americanus

Years from now, when curious anthropologists study the remains of twentieth-century culture, they might rightly conclude that it was the "Great TV-Watching Society." Perhaps they will even create a new Latin phrase for the inhabitants of this media-frenzied culture: *Boobis americanus.* But will they discern the real irony behind this "leisure-rich" culture where everyone was so busy?

According to the Americans' Use of Time Project, the single most dramatic increase in time usage since 1950 surrounds television viewing. The tube now dominates leisure, accounting for 40 percent of adult women's free time and 50 percent of men's. Although women as a group have more leisure time today than they did twenty years ago, *all* of the increased leisure has been dedicated to television, according to Robinson. Nielsen Media Research reports that children and teens watch about three hours daily, and adults over four hours. The typical family has the tube on for over seven hours daily! And these data normally don't include VCRs and video and computer games, only broadcast and cable television.

The intrusion of television into American life has been phenomenal. *TV Guide* reported in 1992 that only 40 percent of Americans would stop watching the tube even for one millon dollars. The study by Peter D. Hart Research Associates also discovered the following:

☐ 63 percent often watch while eating dinner, including 76 percent of those between eight and twenty-four years old

☐ more than a third of viewers leave the set on for background noise

☐ 29 percent fall asleep with the tube on

☐ 42 percent turn on the TV when entering a room

The picture that emerges from these studies probably resembles your family, more or less. We see the tube invading the precious free time of a frenzied culture. Instead of planning how to use the medium, we grab as much "communion" with it as we can while running through life. Research conducted by the J. Walter Thompson organization in 1992 discovered that over 70 percent of viewers of even programs with the greatest viewer loyalty watch only one out of two original episodes monthly. How strange it is that we don't like TV enough to carefully plan our use of it, but we love to fill up so much of our discretionary time with the medium. This is *Boobis americanus.*

As TV viewing has steadily increased, most other leisure activities have decreased. Moviegoing has declined. Reading has decreased by about one-half since the 1960s—especially newspaper reading. Social activities, the second-largest category after TV, still account for about one-quarter of leisure time, but they, too, are decreasing. The simple fact is that television and related media technologies are gobbling up leisure time like no other activities. Leisure seems to disappear, and we frantically search for time to do other things, especially time to build family life.

Most important of all, this media mania directly affects the quantity and quality of family communication. Each new TV technology— cable, remote-control, VCR—increases viewing and erodes family communication. One crosscultural study found that when a household acquires a television, personal communication decreases from about nineteen to around fourteen minutes per day. But in the United States, where TVs are in abundance, the situation is much grimmer. Americans spend between four and five minutes daily conversing with spouses and about thirty seconds with children, according to a report by Fortino & Associates. Estimates suggest that the typical married couple spends about seventeen minutes weekly talking, including such nonrelational remarks as "Please pass the salt" and "Would you take out the garbage?" In a survey conducted for Massachusetts Family Life Insurance Company and *Family Fun* magazine, half of the parents surveyed felt they didn't have enough time with their spouses.

Robinson's studies confirm that parents spend about 40 percent less time with their offspring today than parents did in 1965. He also discovered that the tube indeed detracts from conversation and away-from-home social life, and he suggests that any increases in household communication resulting from television are probably "artificial" rather than genuine and relational. In other words, the typical comment about a TV show or about which channel to watch is not likely to deepen family relations. An interesting study by Robert Kubey found that TV viewing promotes 40 percent less "talking" during the activity than do other family activities.

Because of the crucial importance of family communication in creating loving relationships, these findings should greatly disturb the Christian community. How can a family be anything more than an economic unit without exercising God's marvelous gift of verbal and nonverbal "communion"? Decision Research Corporation found that only 24 percent of adults with incomes over twenty-five thousand dollars reported participating in "companionship"—visiting and talking with friends or spending time with their children. Michael Novak wrote almost two decades ago that many of his college students said they "have hardly ever, or never, had a serious conversation with adults." In an incredible survey at West Calgary (Alberta) Christian School, not one student over grade three listed "doing things together as a family" as a good way to spend free time. Psychiatrist and marriage counselor Pierre Mornell rightly suggests that TV can be a substitute for intimacy between spouses.

I would add that mass media in general can become a poor substitute for deep, rewarding relations with friends and especially family. The problems of *Boobis americanus* are not limited to the television set but extend now to all kinds of new media technologies, from computers to digital audio recordings. Reading, too, can divert people from relationships and give people an excuse not to communicate with family and friends. *Boobis americanus* is a state of mind extending to bookworms, newspaper addicts, magazine freaks, radio junkies and computer hackers. In the new media world, however, the family stakes are greater, because the technologies are so seductive.

The Technological Myth

Behind the rise of *Boobis americanus* is a basic myth that every family should expose: that more technology will automatically enhance leisure time and build family life. I hear men spouting one version of this fallacy all the time—namely, that TV "brings the family together" or that watching the tube is "quality family time." It's amazing how many men use this nutty rationalization to purchase a new TV set before the Super Bowl or to get a higher-tech set with special features like stereo sound or picture-in-a-picture. Americans tend to equate leisure with media gadgetry, thereby creating in their own lives an insatiable appetite for the "good life" that will never be satiated by more technology.

The history of VCR use in most homes will prove my point. Families typically bought VCRs in order to take advantage of the technology's "time-shifting" ability, making it possible to tape TV programs at inconvenient times and view them at convenient ones. Presumably this would help parents spend more time with their children because they could store shows on tape for viewing after the kids were in bed or otherwise unavailable. Also, families could watch television together by playing tapes at mutually convenient times. In short, the family was supposed to be liberated from the tyranny of the broadcast networks' schedules.

Now we know that these benefits were a lot of rhetoric and little real action. Families forgot to set the timers, or in some cases couldn't figure out how to operate them. The whole time-shifting bonanza largely disappeared in most homes, and VCRs became little more than technologies for showing video movies in the home. Reality never matched the mythological promise.

I believe this technological myth is one reason that so many North American homes are media-rich and communication-poor. About one-third of TV sets in the United States are located in bedrooms. Will these devices improve bedroom communication or deepen intimate relations? For many married couples, late nights in bed, after the kids are asleep and chores completed, are among the few times when they can discuss the important events of the day and share some of their deepest joys and concerns.

A Yankelovich survey commissioned by Nickelodeon and *USA Today* found that 45 percent of children in first through tenth grade in the United States had their own television sets. What possible family benefits result from these sets, except reducing conflicts with other family members over which shows will be watched? I can't imagine how personal TV sets for children could enhance or increase family communication, even though they are certainly a *technological* expansion.

The technological myth is based largely on selfish individualism. It assumes that greater media technology for each individual is a benefit for the family and for society. So in the name of leisure fun and technological progress, we load up the family with whatever media gadgets we can afford—or think we can afford. This has resulted in the expansion of media into all kinds of family activities, from vacations to dinnertimes. But it has also meant more time dedicated to audio listening, computer hacking, video games and the like. The latest studies of video-on-demand and pay-per-view services on cable in suburban Denver seem to confirm that these newer technologies will worsen the problem. A spokesman for the cable-TV industry put it this way: "When you make things accessible enough and easy to use, people respond."

Ironically, the technological myth exacerbates the frenzied pace we all abhor. As each family member takes to his or her own technological "de-vices," trying to satiate the need for leisure, the deeper needs of intimacy and identity become even greater. Sharing our lives with distant media celebrities will never satisfy our needs for communion with God and with family and close friends. And the more time we dedicate to the technological personas, the less time we will have for the real people in our midst—the people we supposedly love and serve.

Wives often complain to me in public gatherings about their husbands' seemingly insatiable desire for Sunday sports on television. These husbands might spend four or more hours watching the tube, especially in the fall during football season, and only fifteen or twenty minutes in personal time with their spouses. Given this kind of ritual, it is entirely understandable for a wife to feel that Sundays are for men to relax and for women to take care of the household. Worse yet, some wives get the feeling that their spouses care more about Brent Musberger than they do about their loves ones. These feelings are entirely understandable given the fact that our actions "speak" about who we are and what we believe.

Lonely Children

Our high-tech family lives probably have a bigger impact on children than on spouses. By the time many kids enter school, they've already gotten the message that media are fun and parents are a drag, or that peer groups are joyful and family times are stressful. After all, the media and peers don't place a lot of demands on kids. Parents *expect* particular behaviors, and often they require kids to say or do certain things. As young parents use media to baby-sit children, the kids learn implicitly that the media are acceptable. So why not enjoy the media instead of parents and families?

From the earliest ages, children are socialized by parents to look to the media for leisure. This is true in many single-wage-earner families as well as among dual-wage earners. The Institute for Social Research at the University of Michigan found that *working* moms spent only about eleven minutes on weekdays and a half hour on weekend days in "quality time" with their children (reading to them, conversing and playing with them). Even homemakers spent only thirty minutes daily and thirty-six minutes on weekend days in similar activities. Oddly enough, a Cornell University study found that working mothers spend more time interacting with their three- to five-year-olds than at-home mothers do. Most discouraging of all was the absence of fathers in the lives of their children. Dads dedicate only about eight minutes daily and fourteen minutes on Saturdays or Sundays to their own children. According to a study by the Carnegie Corporation, fathers give five minutes daily to their adolescent children, and only about 5 percent of American children see a grandparent regularly.

Strangely enough, there is a sense of parentlessness even among the children of affluent parents, who simply prefer personal leisure activities to family involvement. This may be one of the reasons that, according to David Myers in *The Pursuit of Happiness,* growing material abundance does not make Americans happier. He finds that close, loving relationships make people much happier than does mere economic success. Real emotional bonding in families, characterized by rich personal interaction and mutual support and encouragement, can't be bought by professional accomplishments. Nor can love be nurtured purely by economic consumption. Family happiness depends on giving one's time to another—time that says "I care about you" and that encourages storytelling, listening and empathizing.

By the period of adolescence, children usually prefer peers and media over time with their own families. We used to talk about the "generation gap," which was really a communication gulf. Now we simply assume the gap because there is so little cross-generational communication in North American culture. Each new generation has its own styles of life and corresponding media preferences. The book *Being Adolescent* reports that youth spend only 7 percent of their waking time with *any* adults, compared with half of their waking hours with peers. Moreover, there's considerable evidence in *The Private Life of the American Teenager* that most adolescents neither consult with nor even communicate with their parents regarding such topics as drugs, relational problems, drinking, sex, and health and diet.

In spite of what adults might like to believe, the breakdown in parent-adolescent communication is not primarily because teenagers are impossible to talk with or because they are badly alienated from their parents. On the contrary, teens say they *want* to communicate first with their parents about important matters in their lives. Adolescents say they are unhappy that adults are not available to listen to them, to empathize with them and to help guide them in life. They look to their peers for popular culture, including what to wear, entertainment and the like, but not for enduring values and beliefs. There is massive evidence that even academic achievement and school performance are related to parental involvement. For these reasons, the Carnegie Council on Adolescent Development suggested that parents and families need to be brought back constructively into adolescents' lives.

Of all age groups, adolescents are among those who have the most discretionary time, but sadly little of it leads to communication with adults. They spend twenty-one hours weekly watching TV, about six hours doing homework and just under two hours reading for pleasure. Like these activities, the rest of their five hours of daily discretionary time is largely unsupervised and unproductive. Many older teenagers work (about two-thirds of all high-school seniors), but most of their coemployees are members of the peer group, especially at fast-food restaurants. Unless they share their lives more deeply and regularly with trusted adults, adolescents will invariably feel more or less lost and lonely in the culture that they will soon inherit.

Squandered Opportunities

As I travel around the country speaking to various groups, I repeatedly hear parental laments about schools and churches. Parents complain about the poor job teachers and pastors are doing at helping to raise their offspring. Meanwhile, some of these same parents are too busy chasing the good life or running after professional success and financial prosperity to raise their own children. No wonder they're disappointed in the performance of *other* adults! It's only natural, under the shadow of the Fall, to blame others for some of our own weaknesses.

Many parents have plenty of leisure time that could be dedicated joyfully to family life and to raising children. But we squander this time on our selfish leisure pursuits, especially the media. As I will suggest in the next chapter, parenting is not simply work or another drain on our limited energy. Parenting can rejuvenate adults, spark joy and even challenge the entertainment value of the best situation comedies.

What kind of legacy would you like to leave behind for your children? Will they remember you as a father or mother who said you loved them but were usually too busy to show that love? Or will they know that you loved them and cherished time with them?

Missing: Rituals of Meaning

One day, sitting in the barber's chair, I initiated a discussion with an acquaintance in the next chair. While we lost a few locks we discussed the latest family news—ages of kids, sicknesses, household chores and so forth. As we got up to leave, I suggested that we meet for coffee some evening to exchange a few more notes on fathering—without the nearby ears of our female barbers. He agreed, but with one firmly stated proviso: "I have to be home by 8:30 p.m. to put my kids to bed. It's a regular ritual, with reading, prayers and hugs. I wouldn't miss it, for one day they'll be gone." That remark was so unusual for one man to say to another that I stood in silence as he walked out the door. I wondered how many fathers could say that about *any* family ritual.

One of the best things about vacations is the freedom to design our own daily schedules. If only life could be like that all year long, without our being unemployed or having to retire! But much of our daily time—more than we think—is already discretionary. The problem is that living in a high-tech campground, we fill our "free" time until it binds us to our own slavish desires for mass-mediated leisure. Then we complain about stress, marital problems and kids gone astray, or just plain gone. All along, *we* were absent from the meaningful relationships that we really wanted but never truly sought.

Family communication takes time, and the only way to find the time is by honestly examining our own lives. Surely our families deserve more of it, and our high-tech "friends" deserve less, even during football season or at the summer campground.

3
Married . . . with Media

Finding Lost Time
& Reclaiming Shared Lives

During my son's posttoddler years we began a father-son tradition that continues to this day: lengthy evening walks together. For years we took turns deciding which routes to take. Living in a city, we have nearly an endless variety of routes, depending on the kinds of neighborhoods we would like to traverse.

When Stephen was about six years old, he requested that we head due north through East Grand Rapids, the most fashionable part of town. I was surprised, because we had never walked that far north before and I hadn't realized that Stephen even knew about this upscale neighborhood. So we donned our best walking clothes and shoes and headed in the proper direction.

I'll never forget the glorious evening of that walk. It had been a warm, sunny fall day, and the cool evening air mixed refreshingly with the radiated warmth of the sun-heated sidewalks. As the sun set, I could smell smoldering leaves from afar, redolent of my childhood in Chicago, when it was legal to gather leaves at the curbside for burning. Along our walkway, a prestigious street lined with enormous oak and sycamore trees, the large leaves fell lazily to the ground around us in the still air. For a moment they looked to me like twenty-dollar bills adorning the gated yards of stately brick and stone homes.

Before long my mind wandered to covetous thoughts about the houses we were passing. Our voices were silent, but my brain imagined my family living in one of these castles with the long driveways, three-season porches, third-floor master bedroom suites and iron gates. The images of wealth contrasted sharply with our actual abode of wood and aluminum siding, with metal corner pieces that blew into the neighbors' yard during thunderstorms. I imagined myself as a resident of an elegant city of stone—an earthly fantasy that can be projected toward every Glencoe or Highland Hills in America.

But suddenly my mental meanderings were eclipsed by an innocent question from my young walking companion: "Dad, are these people going to heaven?"

I was flabbergasted. "What do you mean, son? I really don't know the people of this neighborhood. And you can't judge someone's heart, anyway."

Then his concern took shape: "But look at these big houses and the expensive cars. Doesn't the Bible say that rich people can't get to heaven?"

As night fell and the air grew chilly, Stephen and I began talking about camels, the eyes of needles and the human heart. A covetous father and an innocent young son traded questions and answers as crack after crack of sidewalk passed under our feet. This was no longer just an enjoyable time together, but a spontaneous sharing of two hearts through the gift of communication. Each of us listened, told our stories and empathized with the other, all the way back to our humble but well-loved habitat in another part of town.

These are the kinds of moments that all parents treasure, when the walls between us and our children almost magically disappear and are replaced with trust and understanding. Love flows from such serendipitous events. Teaching and learning occur. Values and beliefs are shared. We experience an earthly communion that builds the networks for future communication and provides the cement for lasting relationships.

How can we "manage" our parental lives to make our family fertile for such deepening relationships? How can we use time to our family's advantage, even in a hectic, stressful world where work and leisure seem to make it nearly impossible? What might we do to transform our families from mere economic organizations into committed, warm and fulfilling groups?

A Low-Tech Strategy
In contemporary North America and other highly industrialized areas, families cannot build until they first destroy. Time is a zero-sum game in our lives. We can't have everything and everyone we want. We simply have to make the hard choices between high-tech media lives and low-tech family relationships. One or the other must be sacrificed for the sake of balanced communication.

For most families, the place to start is not with a wholesale reassessment of lifestyle and work commitments but with a realistic look at leisure time. According to the data, we already have the time for family. Our discussions about changing jobs, moving to different neighborhoods or even working at home are often stalling devices that prohibit us from dealing with the immediate and most changeable issue: selfish attitudes toward leisure. The average adult spends over four hours daily consuming television alone. Until we deal honestly with this fact, it makes little sense getting sidetracked by the complex aspects of the problem.

The place to begin, then, is for every family to embrace a low-tech strategy by limiting high-tech communication. We simply have to put a limit on movies, TV, video games, computers and the like. I suggest about a three-to-one ratio—three parts relational activities to one-part media use. In other words, a family that has roughly four hours daily of leisure or discretionary time would limit high-tech involvement to one hour and low-tech activities to three hours.

If this seems totally unrealistic in your family because of a serious lack of *any* discretionary time, then maybe it is time for a wholesale reassessment of work and other commitments. But I honestly have not yet encountered such a family. In most cases, families wrongly believe that they have no leisure time when in fact they squander large chunks of it every week. If necessary, audit your family time for one week, listing what every family member did for each fifteen-minute block of every day. Chances are you'll be shocked at how radio, movies, computers and especially television monopolize available free time.

The three-to-one rule will work well only if the high-tech time is the same for all family members. For example, in my home we seriously limit television to one hour daily. If each of us selects a different program, we may never gather together for family activities. So either some of us have to decide not to use our high-tech hour or we all have to tape our shows and view them on different sets during the same leisure hour. As I'll discuss in the next chapter, we've never found the latter a very acceptable option, because we prefer to do much of our viewing together. So we often negotiate over which shows to make family "events," thereby even dedicating high-tech time to a low-tech purpose—namely, common viewing and discussion. Other times we pair up, with two or more of us reading and discussing the same book or article, going to a movie togeth-er or playing a computer game. The trick is to limit media time, which is never acceptable as real family time even though families may spend it together.

Some of my more literate friends wrongly think that they can promote deep family relationships merely by limiting TV viewing. In their eyes the tube is the devil, while reading is often the implied savior of family life. So they encourage parents to read instead of watch television. For all of the potential benefits of reading—a heightened imagination, in-creased vocabulary, more verbal fluency and so on—this strategy is no better for family life than wide-open television viewing. Reading is not as high-tech as the VCR, but both of them can be serious roadblocks to transforming leisure time into a resource for building family life. Book lovers beware! Periodical addicts take note! Long before *Boobis america-nus* there was *Printus americanus*. Bob Keeshan, also known as Captain Kangaroo, put it this way: "Parents have to wake up and decide that their children come before work, recreation, social relationships or anything else. Until that happens, we'll pay the price."

Since television is the biggest consumer of leisure time, however, most of us should indeed look first to the tube for new family time. Gordon Nikel, writing on "The Joys of a TV-Free Summer" in *Focus on the Family* magazine, recalls how his family discovered that "life without TV, far from being a negative experience . . . frees an astounding amount of time for building relationships with people, for furthering a Christian witness in the neighborhood, and for filling the mind with thoughts and images of God and His Kingdom." These are some of the benefits of a low-tech strategy in family communication.

Quality Time

The term *quality time* is so widely—and wrongly—used these days that

I fear some readers might skip this section of the book. So don't assume you know what quality time really is. Leah Walloch and Amy Dombro persuasively argue in *The Ordinary Is Extraordinary* that quality time ought not to be equated with special activities, for fear that parents will fail to see the value of everyday living as a chance to communicate with children. If our quality time with offspring is only special events or occasions, separated from the rest of life, we've lost most of the real opportunities for building family relationships and teaching our children. It's too easy for all of us busy parents to pretend that a little "quality time" can substitute for "quantity time," as Katrina Gettman put it.

Quality time is not only the special, isolated moments when time has been formally set aside for parent-child or spouse-spouse interactions. It is also the time family members spend doing other things together—working at home, riding in the car, shopping, cooking. Such times are "quality" when the activities themselves are not the full focus, when interpersonal communication emerges naturally during the course of day-to-day events.

For years my wife has worked in the kitchen with our growing daughter. Sometimes they plan ahead to prepare particular meals, make Christmas cookies or bake special treats for school celebrations. But more often than not they simply decide at the last minute to whip together some food for the family. As they gather ingredients and taste their concoctions, they laugh and learn about each other as well as about cooking. My wife talks about her mother and her family experiences in and out of the kitchen. Our daughter delights in those stories and responds with her own special tales of cooking and eating at friends' houses, at summer camp and everywhere else.

Compared with many other activities, television viewing and video games can be particularly destructive of this type of family time, because they inhibit the potential for communication. If we glance away from the set, we might miss part of the program. Similarly, if we talk with or even listen to another person while the set is on, we'll lose some of the show. VCRs can make viewing more flexible, but most families will not take the time to tape regular TV programs in advance. Time-bound video games are even worse. One of the most disturbing places for me is a video arcade, where there is virtually no real human communication amidst the cacophony of electronic sounds and the entranced faces of the players and observers.

The following guidelines for family communication will promote real quality time.

1. Don't force it. Parents often mistakenly try to force communication with each other and with their children. Unless there is truly an emergency that absolutely demands communication, time is best left open. When threats or verbal anger is used to force children to communicate, they may not say what they really feel but rather what they think the parents expect or want to hear. The result is decreased trust on both sides. The greater pressure children feel, the harder it is for them to understand and express themselves. A parent's respect for a child is often best expressed by permitting silence and offering nonverbal signs of encouragement, such as holding hands, patting on the back and smiling.

This is one of the major reasons I like walking with my son. Neither of us feels that we *have* to talk as we walk. If thoughts come to mind, we might express them, but always because we desire to communicate. I've tried never to use the walks as a time to interrogate my son about school, his friends or anything else. I have, however, frequently asked general questions merely as a reminder that I'm available for discussion: "How was your day?" "How are things going?" even "How am I doing as your father?"

2. Let it develop gradually. Even when the situation is right for open communication, progress is often slow. Young children need time to figure out their emotions, while older ones need time to accept and admit them. As children mature, they become more verbally fluent about their experiences. But they also suffer, like adults, with self-doubts and worries about what others think of them. A gradual opening up of parent-child communication is entirely normal. After all, even between adult spouses it can take a long while for quality time to lead to deep and authentic communication.

3. Do more listening than speaking. Communication is best accomplished when the most fluent and dominant party spends more time listening rather than speaking. Too many parents do exactly the opposite, bombarding their children with messages. The resulting message overload teaches children to blast back rather than to listen and empathize. Also, it makes parents falsely believe that they have actually communicated *with* their children when they have only really spoken *at* them.

Even when children find it hard to speak with their parents, they need to know that their parents are willing to listen. By making ourselves available as listeners, we implicitly say to our children that we love them and value them. In effect, we give them our time and make their emotional needs our own concerns—just by turning an open ear.

The spirituality of listening is hard to fathom unless we recognize the example we have in Christ, who encourages us to pray about everything and promises that he will *always* listen. What would our relationship with Christ be like if we never knew whether his ears were turned our way? Children can have such doubts, not just about Christ but about their parents: "Do they really listen to me? Do they really care?" This is why it is so important for us to spend quality time listening to the stories of those whom we want to love. Without listening, there will not be much trust, let alone understanding and love.

4. Do it regularly. Family communication needs to be done with regularity, not in a haphazard fashion. As parents and spouses, we need to make ourselves available at regular times and places so that communication is comfortable and expected. Again, like communion with God, communication with each other grows incrementally when it is practiced. It simply doesn't work to get into fits of open communication for a while and then revert to selfish uses of personal time. Regularity is essential.

In my view, daily family communication is very important for building deep, trusting relationships. Even when I'm out of town, I call home around bedtime to assure the family that I care about them. Usually each person gets a chance to speak with me on the phone, and I spend more time asking questions and listening than I do jabbering about work or the places I'm staying. A number of years ago I even decided that rather than leaving the family behind I would, whenever possible, take them along. This way we could continue some of our daily communication rituals even while I was on the road. I also began turning down a number of speaking opportunities because they involved travel without my family.

5. Make it part of your daily activities. Signs at the Indianapolis Children's Museum say, "Talk and think about what you see at the museum today." The best communication springs naturally from our daily activities. My wife and I have discovered that practically everything we do with our family is an opportunity for building quality time. Among the most common activities are eating meals, driving in the car, shopping, yard and house work, and snack times. For my wife and our daughter, bread baking is especially good because of all the time spent working the dough and letting it rise. Each of these activities is fertile ground for the seeds of family bonds. Again, during these times we ask questions, tell our stories, listen and empathize. It's fun and rewarding.

But beware: these types of activities are not easily preserved as opportunities for communication. Meals are increasingly approached like fast-food "gulp-downs," if not like TV-viewing events. I'll never forget the time during college that a girlfriend first invited me to dinner to meet her family. Upon arrival, we were ushered quickly and quietly into the kitchen, where the entire family sat silently around the table as they watched the news, weather and sports on a countertop set. I had no choice but to join the audience.

Car trips are often filled with radio or taped music. Shopping is done either alone or at such a frenetic pace that communication is nearly impossible. Housework is typically so compartmentalized that family members take care of their individual responsibilities at their own discretion. Fewer and fewer homes seem to make family time even for these types of activities.

I learned when my children were quite young that they love to do "work" with parents if they get attention in the process. So I began cleaning the kitchen or washing the car with one or both of the kids. Sometimes it was frustrating because I spent more time teaching the kids what to do, or cleaning up after them, than I did accomplishing the task at hand. But in the long run the benefits of this approach to daily life are clearly evident. We enjoy doing things together, and Dad's impatience and the kids' messiness are relatively accepted—and joked-about—parts of every job. Even during housework we learned to discuss our weaknesses, and to do so with love and understanding.

Special Times

If daily communication is in relatively good order, families can benefit considerably from special activities designed to promote warm and loving relationships. Remember, however, that things rarely work in the opposite direction. When daily communication is a mess, strained by lack of trust and unwillingness to listen, special activities will often *increase* stress and further debilitate family members. Never try putting all your hopes for improved communication into one outing, a carefully planned vacation or a special dinner together. More often than not, you'll be disappointed.

On the other hand, when daily family interaction is usually fun as well as relationship-building, special times can be set aside productively to build relationships among parents and children. During the last few years I've collected suggestions from dozens of adults and children. Usually I've asked one major question: "What special activities were most important while you were growing up for building healthy family relationships?" The responses are interesting as well as helpful to all of us who would like to learn from others.

Board games (and some video/computer games). Many parents mention this activity, but very few children. I can only surmise that video games and television have made these types of games relatively obsolete, except for the occasional fad like Trivial Pursuit, a few classics like Monopoly and Scrabble, and updated folk games like Balderdash (one of our favorites for sheer inanity). Nevertheless, board games are still a viable means for promoting family communication. I dare you to try to play one and to talk only about the game!

Some video and computer games offer the same benefits as board games. Multiplayer games that are not time-bound can promote family communication. Unfortunately, most video games are designed for one player and are strongly based on accomplishing a task in a limited time. Players "communicate" with the machine more than they do with other players. Fortunately, it appears that computer program manufacturers are more committed to family games, as I'll discuss more in the next chapter.

Vacations. A large number of baby boomers say that vacations were perhaps the most important family times in their childhood and adolescent years. My wife is one of them. Her auto trips crisscrossing the United States with family were among the most relaxing and relational times of her formative years. So I am distressed to see that many married boomers are now abandoning family vacations and replacing them with couples' vacations as a means of getting away from the kids. If vacations are indeed formative times for family development, they ought not to be used only for rejuvenating marriages.

As essay on this topic in *The New York Times* stressed the value of travel for building relationships between teens and their parents. A travel writer who journeys with her children warned, "Unless you travel with your teenagers, your time with them is likely to be limited to swapping car keys and telephone messages. . . . It's a chance for you to get to know each other as people. Your kids get to see you as a person, not just a parent." While her observation may be a bit exaggerated, it still makes a lot of sense. Vacations do remove teens from their peer group and give parents the opportunity to spend much more time with them than they would at home.

As our children entered adolescence, we began involving them increasingly in the planning of family vacations. This way they could "own" the vacation and not feel as if they were being dragged by their parents to boring activities or "adult" places. The result has been particularly rewarding for us, because we get away from not only work but also the daily media distractions that can gobble up spare time. Our media use declines considerably during vacations, while our personal communication increases manyfold. My wife often tells us during vacations of the times she and her family visited the same places.

Sports. The frequency of this activity in people's lists greatly surprised me, partly because my own parents rarely played sports with me and partly because I didn't see sports as very conducive to interpersonal communication. The key, apparently, is the type of sports activity. Among the most frequently mentioned sports are golf, horseback riding, winter skiing, hunting, fishing and swimming. These all involve considerable free time, unlike a competitive team sport such as basketball.

Based partly on these findings, my wife and I began to invest more time and energy—not to mention money—in helping our kids become more proficient in noncompetitive sports that they might share with their own children. Certainly there are other benefits to sports, such as greater self-confidence and exercise. But the relational benefits alone are enough to convince us that our children should be encouraged and enabled to participate in sports.

Hobbies. Again, I didn't expect to find this category in people's lists of family-building activities. In my childhood, hobbies were individualized among family members, and none of us participated much in others' hobbies. We respected each other's hobbies, but not to the point of doing them together.

The variety of hobbies is practically endless, but some of them come up over and over again: gardening, collecting, pets and cooking. It seems to me that most hobbies are likely to attract older children, while sports will usually interest younger ones. I've done a lot of gardening, but our kids have never expressed much interest in participating, except when it comes time for major landscaping around the house. When they were younger, they liked to dig holes and mix the dirt, as well as to put the plants into the ground. My wife has had far more success with cooking, which appeals considerably to our daughter. The two of them have spent many afternoons and evenings preparing treats for special occasions and house guests. In the process, they converse about all kinds of things, including some of the most intimate mother-daughter topics.

If a child shows an interest in a new hobby, it is probably worth pursuing as a possible parent-child activity. Most of the time hobbies are faddish interests or unfeasible for one reason or another. A while back my son mentioned that he'd like to try remote-control flying. So we went to a local hobby shop and found an extremely helpful salesperson who carefully explained to us the ins and outs of this popular activity. Given the financial investment, the weather needs, the necessity of a fairly close but protected field and the lack of mentor-friends who knew anything about the hobby, we decided not to get involved at that time. Since then, however, we've discovered neighbors and friends who are involved in remote-control clubs, and we might change our minds, especially if my son is serious enough to commit some of his hard-earned cash to the pastime.

But you never know what will most interest kids. When I got involved a few years ago in a relatively obscure ham-radio hobby called fox-hunting, I invited my son along on a lark. He got more interested than I was in the hobby, which involves tracking down hidden transmitters with the use of directional antennas, maps, compasses and a lot of luck. He started recommending places to hide transmitters and began studying for his own amateur radio license. Before long I found that we could easily chat about the hobby, and those conversations became springboards for all kinds of discussions. In addition, we went together to after-the-hunt social activities, which gave him a good opportunity to practice the friendly art of conversation with other adults, yet with the safety of my company.

Food and talk. Food and conversation have long gone together, so I was not surprised that many people said food outings were important family activities. I was pleasantly surprised, however, to learn that some parents spend special times with their children at restaurants. Food, like movies and shopping, is sometimes a pleasant excuse to socialize with people we enjoy. Why not use our appetite for culinary delights to help fill our hunger for loving relationships?

My wife and I learned the benefits of table conversation during our courting years while I was a graduate student in Champaign-Urbana, Illinois. A friend introduced us to an inexpensive Korean restaurant in a downtown area, far enough from campus and my wife's work that we could retire there for discussion without interruptions from either my fellow graduate students or her coworkers. The rest of the world stood still when we entered the doorway of this modest place. It was just the two of us, on either side of the table, sharing our daily triumphs and tragedies as well as our long-term dreams and fears. As time went on, our discussions started to cover some of the deepest matters of heart and soul. Eventually we were married in that city where a back-alley restaurant had provided the time and place for us to commune.

Years later, we see the value of those table chats, and we frequently invoke the name of our favorite restaurant in Grand Rapids as a symbol for relational conversation. Not surprisingly, each of us takes our children there, sometimes together and other times individually, to discuss matters of the heart and soul as well as to converse about the important but mundane stuff of everyday life. And we often stop in at the same restaurant after seeing movies or attending local plays and concerts together. The food is great, but far more important are the storytelling, listening and empathizing.

Christian service activities. Only a few families have mentioned this idea, but it seems like such a good one that I hope others will try it as well. Some families donate a regular portion of their time to a Christian service activity that promotes family life as well as helps other people. They might work together at the local food distribution center, for instance, providing nonperishable items for needy families. Parent-child teams might contribute Saturday mornings to Habitat for Humanity projects. Obviously there are many possibilities for this type of "quality time."

The Male Problem

Whenever I discuss these matters in public, I am invariably challenged by skeptical men who see things very differently. Generally speaking, men are less open to people's relational needs and more interested in technological gadgetry, including media. To them it doesn't seem very manly to plan time for communication or to talk about emotional needs. When I suggest that men watch too much television and that watching the tube with children is not quality time, they often turn on me as if I'm a traitor to the male cause. In their eyes, they *deserve* evenings and weekends loaded with televised football, mealtimes behind a newspaper and auto trips accompanied by radio sports.

All of this is a serious problem for the North American family. The truth is that even when fathers and husbands are physically present in the house, many of them do not make themselves very available to their spouses and children. Some of the statistics in the previous chapter show how little time men spend with the people they supposedly love. More significant is the fact that men are not committed to quality time, because they are less likely to feel the need for it themselves or to see the need for it in spouses and children.

So I would ask the men reading this book to examine their own lives. Are you aware of your family's emotional needs? Do you know what's on the minds and in the hearts of your spouse and children today? What fears face your sons and daughters? What does your family most like and dislike about you? Do you spend as much time communing with your family as you do pursuing your own leisure activities, including media use? If you can't answer these questions with certainty, you probably need to reestablish communication with your loved ones.

Men offer me primarily one excuse (really a rationalization) for their selfish behavior: They use the media to relax and unwind after a hard day's work. In short, they deserve to put themselves first after working so hard "for the family." This kind of excuse simply doesn't work, because the money they contribute to the family will never alone meet their wife and children's greater need for love. No leisure-time device—whether cottage, boat, RV or remote-control television—will quench the family's thirst for understanding, acceptance and encouragement.

Therefore, I believe it is very important in this consumer-oriented society for men to learn to relax through low-tech means of interpersonal interaction. The suggestions offered in this chapter are good places to begin, but fathers need to be creative enough to find the activities that will both help them unwind and promote unforced, unrushed communication with the family. Love is not just the absence of abusive actions or negative communication, but the selfless presence of one person in the life of another.

The Church Problem

If males are a roadblock to reclaiming family life, so is the local church. I wish it weren't true. And I wish I didn't feel compelled to discuss this issue on these pages. My goal is not to criticize pastors or other church leaders, but to point out how the church has succumbed to some worldly ways of organization that work against the needs of the family.

First, too many churches carve up the family into individual members of different groups. I'll never forget the time my wife and I visited a new church for the first time. We showed up on a Wednesday evening for "family night." A cordial fellow greeted us at the door with instructions regarding where each member of the family would go if indeed we had children. Both of us quickly realized what was happening: family night wasn't a time for the family to come together, but an evening for individual family members to do different things with nonfamily in the same building.

Without challenging the need for age-oriented or even gender-oriented activities in congregations, I would simply point out that churches spend far more time splitting up families than they do bringing them together, except for worship. Therefore, I would like to encourage churches to sponsor some of the types of activities suggested in this chapter. In my opinion, even youth groups invest too much time in adolescent activities and too little in family ones.

Second, churches often unknowingly encourage members, especially men, to be overcommitted to congregational activities. This both turns church life into additional stressful work and keeps church workers away from their families. The authors of *Toxic Faith* even suggest that church activities can seriously interfere with a godly family life. Here again, the church needs to be considerably more creative about promoting family life.

Riding the River

Time, the philosopher once said, is like a river. You can never put your feet in the same water twice. Once time rushes downriver, it's gone for good.

As we get older, we see anew the river of our past, and we reconsider how best to spend our time. Perhaps this is why, according to a University of Michigan study, people aged fifty-five to sixty-four give more of their time to their families (150 hours annually) than any other age group. Could it be that they have learned the value of family life relative to work and other leisure pursuits? The older we get, the more clearly we see the errors of our past. It's not unusual for parents to wish that they had given more of themselves to their children before the young ones left the nest.

As I walked with my son through the neighborhood of elegant homes, I pondered the importance of this simple activity in his life. Surely he would remember these evening journeys around the city. Someday when he was a father he might recall some of those precious moments together—times like the trip through East Grand Rapids, when we communed through our talk of camels and needles. Whichever treks he remembered, he would most likely recall the fact that I was there with him, listening to his stories and reliving my own childhood through his experiences. Now I imagine him strolling down a street of huge palaces with his own little son walking alongside him and feeling like a king.

4
A Different World

Getting a Handle on the
New Media Technologies

In late 1992 a Muslim group opposed to importing satellite "dish" antennas in Kuwait reportedly distributed the following note on the city's doorsteps:

> In the name of Allah the Compassionate, the Merciful, beware of the herpes and AIDS satellite dish. . . . Take a vow not to let this device get into your household. . . . Can you trust that your wife, sons, and daughters are immune to the forces that destroy religion, honor, and ethics? . . . What was once impossible has become commonplace because of the Western media invasion.

A young Muslim housewife offered a telling response to the satellite threat: "Those who want to go to the mosque can go and those who want to have fun can have fun."

When I first read those opposing views of satellite television, I was dumbfounded. How is it that arguments about new media technologies in the Arab Middle East could echo the debates in North America? The answer, of course, is that all families in industrialized nations feel essentially the same tensions—tensions between religion and secularism, morality and immorality, traditional ways of life and modern ways, family and outside world, high-tech and low-tech. In Kuwait the "bad guys" might be in the West, whereas in North America they might be in Hollywood, New York or Toronto. But there are always bad guys and good guys who seek our trust, our pocketbooks and our allegiance.

Because the Fall cast a shadow over humankind's "naming" of the world, communications technology is a hotly disputed subject in religious circles. Since media are always in the identity business, they are usually supercharged topics of cultural conflict. This was true of printing, movies and broadcasting. Now it's true of everything from satellites to computers and video games.

In earlier books, *Redeeming Television* and *Televangelism and American Culture,* I suggested that Christians have to avoid two extremes. One is the temptation to believe that new media technologies are nothing but tools of the devil. Parents who take this approach are likely to discover a growing gulf between themselves and their increasingly media-savvy children, who have probably discovered some worthwhile uses for the new technologies. The other unacceptable extreme is to mindlessly adopt every new technological invention as if it will necessarily make life better and lead to unparalleled pleasure.

This chapter takes the middle ground by searching for appropriate and God-glorifying uses for the new technologies, as well as by cautioning against known drawbacks. I try to offer some "prophetic" wisdom about these media, not in the sense of grand predictions about the fate of those who do or don't adopt these technologies, but in the sense of wisdom gleaned from applying the Scriptures to the lessons of history and the realities of the current situation.

Generally speaking, I've learned that new technologies spread faster than one would expect but rarely produce the marvelous benefits predicted. In the 1980s, for example, personal computers spread rapidly across North America, but they never really streamlined household chores or gave families a lot more leisure time. Similarly, cellular telephones now dot the tops of automobiles and trucks up and down the highways, but I doubt that they have considerably improved most people's work or leisure time. In fact, they can often be an irritating intrusion into discussion and contemplation.

Nevertheless, these and other technologies can contribute to godly and rewarding family life when they are used sensibly and discerningly. So here we go, down the wild racetrack of communications technologies. Buckle your seat belts, and make sure your spiritual air bags are ready for any sudden crashes. After all, your family's on board a fast-moving vehicle.

What's Out There, E.T.?

The modern world is loaded with developing, merging and derivative media technologies. Practically every month we hear, see or read about some "new" breakthrough. Some of these reports are relatively accurate but carefully orchestrated news "plants" designed to garner support from corporate stockholders. Others are overly optimistic predictions by wide-eyed but undereducated journalists. Still others are alarming but half-baked tales of impending woe, such as the stories about cellular phones' causing brain cancer among users. I call this wacky montage of today's media world "E.T.," short for *elusive technology*. Media tend to elude the grasp of popular writers and broadcasters who claim to teach us "the way it is."

So in a nutshell, here's the way it *really* is—I think: miniaturized construction and so-called digital electronics have potentially made it easier, more efficient and less costly for a greater number of people to communicate with more people than ever before. The key words are *digital*, *communicate* and *potentially*.

Digital simply refers to a new way of electronically storing and transmitting data, or really any information, including images, text and sounds. Instead of storing such information on cave walls, on parchment or on paper, we can now do it "on" electronic parts called chips. Computers, including the minicomputer in your TV remote control and the one in your memory telephone, are collections of these chips with connecting wires and electronic circuits designed to make them work.

Communicate refers to the way the information (or "data") in these chips can be used. Imagine the chips as enormous filing cabinets loaded with written documents and audio and video recordings. Chips make it very easy to copy all of that stuff in the cabinets very quickly and to deliver the cabinets to someone else in almost no time. Whether anyone will read, view or listen to the stuff, however, depends on their time and interest. So the modern "communications" revolution does not necessarily guarantee more or better communication, only more and better *transmission*. As we shall see, the new technologies often promise improved communication but typically only deliver more *potential* communication.

More than any previous time in history, the family faces an impending communications overload resulting from the abundance of digitally transmitted messages. All of the older media, from the printed page to audio recordings, television and the telephone, are slowly being converted into digital message-bearers.

A computer, for example, does this with anything we "type" into it. One result is that I can now send copies of that typed message to one hundred or more of my colleagues around the world in a matter of seconds, if they have the proper electronic equipment. Of course they may never read or otherwise use the message. Similarly, I could open a business (others are already working on this) where I sell musical compact discs (CDs) for *any* recordings ever made, without ever stocking a single one! In fact, my store can be the size of a large telephone booth. When a customer calls or comes to the shop to order the recording, I call up my distributor, who sends the recording electronically to me over the phone. The tunes are instantaneously copied onto a CD, and the customer rushes home with the CD in hand.

None of this is pie-in-the-sky dreaming. It's a small part of the elusive technological revolution brought on by changes in electronics, especially the digital chip. More "things" can *potentially* be *communicated* to more people more quickly than ever before.

Where's the Beef?

What are the practical implications of this new digital media world? How will it get into our homes? How will we likely use it? Over the next few years more and more families will find this electronic world in their homes. Here are the major developments we can expect.

1. Hundreds of TV channels. We'll probably have several-hundred-channel systems within a few years. It *will* happen, because the cable-TV and telephone companies see more business in more channels, whether they are transmitted to the home through space or, more likely, via fiber-optic, telephone or coaxial cables. If you're wondering who would have the time for all of these channels, consider this: in 1992 alone Americans rented 3.6 billion videos, purchased 73 million video games and spent $21.5 billion on cable TV.

My guess is that most of the new channels will offer one of the following: (1) specialized sports, (2) movies, (3) concerts, (4) genre entertainment (for example, all Westerns, all game shows, all live-talk shows), (5) international programs from all around the world, (6) greater live "news" coverage, (7) political or ideological programming, (8) lifestyle programming for leisure pursuits, such as boating and golfing, (9) probably other "lifestyle" programming according to certain values, such as gay or lesbian programs or more specialized religious fare, and (10) age-specific programming, such as cartoons for kids and teen-oriented drama.

Undoubtedly there will be "choices" available to subscribers, and likely most of the channels will be offered as pay or pay-per-view services. And the channels will be "packaged" creatively in an effort to get viewers to purchase programming that they might not want.

As the channels expand, the quality of video and audio on television will improve. We should expect more and better stereo as well as greatly improved video images, including increasingly larger images. These developments will turn the home into a movie theater. In fact, we see this already in some of the new residential architecture, which provides entertainment or audio-video rooms with space for a large-screen television, few or no windows, and plenty of storage for video and audio equipment.

2. More audio choices. New communications technologies will also lead to an explosion in radio "stations" and audio recordings. In the United States, the AM radio band will be expanded in an already saturated market—many existing AM stations are in financial trouble. More important is the development of subscription radio delivered to homes via cable, fiber optics or even satellites. These will be high-quality signals, the best fidelity available for avid listeners. And most of the programming will likely be very selective: specialized jazz, oldies, ethnic, opera, Broadway and other styles of music. Since this type of "radio" will be sold on a subscription basis, it will probably be commercial-free—at least initially.

But the biggest revolution in audio will certainly be digital recording and copying. In short, consumers will quickly be able to make *perfect* copies of existing recordings on reusable discs. This will be a far cry from the slow and imperfect system of audiotapes, in which each copy is inferior to the original and variations in tape speed and quality sometimes even produce unacceptable copies.

As I suggested earlier in the chapter, on-site digital copying will largely change the way retail audio sales are conducted. Stores will be able to make perfect copies of original recordings listed in computerized catalogs. Of course these stores might still stock multiple copies of current hit recordings, but they could become retail providers of *any* audio recordings ever made. The concept of an "out-of-print" recording might become outdated. One telephone call or a simple computer transaction could produce a "perfect" copy of any audio recording ever converted to digital technology. Audio's growth, then, will roughly parallel television's expansion, with more products that seem ever more realistic.

3. The growth of electronic gaming. Because of the phenomenal success of the Nintendo and Sega games in the late 1980s and early 1990s, most parents now recognize that electronic gaming is not an isolated fad. Certainly particular games and electronic systems will come and go, but electronic gaming is here to stay. All other forms of household play will be challenged by the electronic revolution. In the early 1990s the video-game industry actually surpassed the movie box office as a source of entertainment revenue. By the end of the century video games will likely be as common in homes as VCRs. There are even some indications that movie videos will themselves become interactive, permitting viewers to select plot lines and story endings.

Electronic games combine audio and video in an *interactive* format, where the player interacts with the game itself and in some cases with other players. This interactive quality makes electronic gaming far more attractive to most kids than board games, card games or even simple imaginative play. In addition, these digital games often include levels of difficulty so players can always find their match. Finally, since they're usually designed to be played without a partner, electronic games require no social expertise or even any social commitments. One does not need friends to play them. In a sense, they're the ultimate game for an individualistic land of bored loners.

Needless to say, electronic gaming will take advantage of all the developments in television and audio technologies, as well as advances in computers. Every few years there will be new game systems that are more impressive and perhaps more addictive than previous ones. Some people even believe that these games will soon approach *virtual reality*, a highly sophisticated state of visual and aural representation where the player feels like he or she is in another world, not just in a game. Indeed, with binocularlike eyepieces and quality headphones it is now possible to create a remarkably real world for players. At this stage, however, the virtual-reality world is not adequately interactive for the player to suspend all disbelief in the electronic images and sounds.

Electronic gaming is expanding in multiple directions. These include smaller games for personal use during travel or boring moments in a chair at home. My son and daughter play a miniaturized game provided in their orthodontist's waiting room, although the volume control has been glued in the "off" position so other patients and parents are not irritated by the goofy electronic sounds. Games are also getting more sophisticated to attract older players. Some games are specifically designed for their educational benefits, such as learning history, geography, math and problem-solving. More and more family-oriented games are on the market, too, but this is admittedly not the biggest market for these electronic products, which appeal overwhelmingly to school-age and adolescent boys. These kids often prefer the more violent, action-oriented games.

4. The spread of electronic mail. If all of this is not very confusing so far, hold on to your remote control! We are at the beginning of a major revolution in *electronic* mail—messages delivered electronically from one computer to another. Many schools and businesses are already using this technology within and between offices, and more and more homes are joining the revolution.

Digital messages can be sent instantaneously over wires, through the airways and via glasslike fiber-optic cables. Right now most homes and offices are using telephone lines to send and receive these messages. Family members usually call a local phone number to connect their computer to one of the international "information services," such as CompuServe or America On-Line, or to local "bulletin board" services. These services, in turn, enable the family member to send messages to friends, relatives or acquaintances in the neighborhood and around the world. Messages go through an enormous computer provided by the information service, which electronically routes them to the appropriate party on the receiving end. Family members call the service to receive their messages on a home computer. The entire procedure is not much more complicated than typing a message or making a phone call. Moreover, it can be cheaper and faster than sending paper letters. Normally it takes only seconds to send a message across the country or even around the world.

Electronic mail would not be very revolutionary except for its broader implications. In addition to exchanging personal letters, families that sign up for "e-mail" will increasingly be able to send and receive just about anything that can be put in digital form—which means nearly any text, sound or image. In addition, the rise of e-mail signals the development of a new kind of world where practically *every* type of human communication could be made electronic. In other words, nearly everything that currently requires in-person or at least person-to-person communication could potentially take place via computer. This might include shopping, banking, library research or browsing, some forms of education, gaming and the like.

The most important development for leisure time will be the use of e-mail to exchange practically all types of media products. One can already receive computer games, video images, audio recordings and periodicals via e-mail. As computers, software (computer programs) and transmission "cables" develop, it will be entirely possible to order and receive virtually every type of media product directly into the home. This is not a nutty prognostication or far-fetched science fiction. This is the media world our children are now inheriting.

5. An explosion in personal communication. Already we see how laptop computers, cellular telephones and personal pagers are changing work and leisure. These technologies are just the beginning of a major revolution in personal communication that will put more and more individuals in instant communication with other individuals regardless of where they are located. It is not inconceivable that by the turn of the century millions of residents of industrialized societies will carry miniaturized "telephones" in their pockets or purses, putting them at the immediate beck and call of anyone who has their number, anywhere around the world.

This explosion in personal communication may be the most significant of all technological developments in media, because it has the

potential to affect so directly all of our relationships. Unless we decide
to limit the technology to work applications, it can invade every aspect
of our lives, from childrearing to leisure pursuits. In the old Dick
Tracy comics the crime fighter was always "in touch" with others via
his wrist radio. That may have been good for nabbing criminals, but
was it good for Tracy's personal life?

The Home as a Stop on the Electronic Highway

The old expression about the home as a "castle" makes little sense
in the new electronic world. Castles were surrounded by moats, protected by massive walls and doors, and guarded by militia. The guards
could rather easily regulate who entered the gates and thereby could
control much of the castle's communication with the outside world.
Whether this was good for the people inside depended, of course, on
the extent of external threats as well as the level of benevolence of
the ruler of the estate. Horses, human feet and boats largely limited
communication, a word that meant nearly the same thing as *transportation* (except for homing pigeons).

As the media developed, beginning with the printing press and the
resulting Protestant Reformation, castles were decreasingly isolated.
The printed word began a long communications revolution that we've
inherited in an electronic form. Communication is more rapid and
ubiquitous today than Martin Luther and the other Reformers could
ever have imagined. Now all social institutions—all churches, corpo-
rations, schools and nations—face being undermined by the nearly
uncontrollable flow of messages through space and across geographic
and political boundaries.

Obviously the entire world is not equally wired in to this electronic
network, and there will always be companies, religions and political
leaders who seek to control people's access, for good and bad reasons.

But the new electronic superhighways are rapidly being constructed around the globe.

In this type of world, the home is not a castle but a stop along the electronic highway, a kind of digital bus stop or airport terminal where people enter and leave the house. Even if we are living in a place that is safe from *physical* harm, we increasingly reside along a highway with a remarkable potential for emotional damage or, more broadly, cultural influence. These superhighways are enormous conduits for transmitting and receiving culture. In creational terms, they are highly developed technologies for naming who we are, how we would like to live and what kind of world we will leave for future generations.

If I am right about the design of the coming media world—and I believe that my descriptions are imminent realities—then families face wonderful opportunities as well as serious dangers along this electronic highway. Here are some of the major issues parents and children will have to face, preferably with the assistance of churches and schools.

Cultural chaos. So many messages will be available that cultural abundance will be a considerable threat to maintaining stable values and beliefs in a rapidly changing world. Imagine turning a child loose in a vast candy store. To some extent, cable television has already created this situation for couch potatoes. Children often respond to televisual abundance by zapping their remote controls, bouncing from one channel to the next. None of the programs is taken particularly seriously; they're all "just TV," just one more product quickly considered and abandoned—a few chips from this bag, pretzels from another and popcorn from yet another.

This type of market-oriented, technology-driven cultural abundance turns culture into a cacophony of mixed messages, disparate values and beliefs, and rapidly changing experiences. On the media highway there isn't any center or core, no eternal compass or absolute reference point. Nor will we see or hear any clear worldview or identifiable cosmology as the messages fly past our eyes and ears. How will we get a handle on this high-tech traffic?

Cultural chaos will also be created by enormously sophisticated audience segmentation. Again, we see the beginnings of this in contemporary radio and cable TV, where there seems to be a channel for just about everyone, from teens to upscale movie fans. But imagine a future scenario of even more specialized television, radio, periodicals, games, travel information, political ideology, diet fads, clothing and all the rest.

Historian Daniel Boorstin in *The Americans: The Democratic Experience* described North America as a land of "consumption communities" where people have more in common with others who purchase and display the same consumer goods than they do even with friends, neighbors, fellow church congregants or members of the same political parties. The electronic highway will hasten this process by linking individual people to the same messages. Our friends, colleagues and acquaintances will be found increasingly along the highway rather than through communication "in the flesh." Moreover, we will tend to identify ourselves with others who consume the same media products rather than with those who grew up in the same neighborhood, attend the same church or live in the same area. Our son talks about wanting to meet his "friends" from one of the local computer bulletin boards, when in fact he's conversed with many of these folks over only the electronic keyboard.

The creation of ever more specialized audiences will constantly push the limits of socially acceptable standards. There will be money to be made by feeding the desires of sinful people on the fringes. We see this already with so-called sex-talk telephone services and adult cable and satellite channels. The electronic superhighway lets even less easily distinguishable small groups organize themselves across geographic space by exchanging messages and purchasing and selling specialized products. It might be financially and logistically difficult for neo-Nazi skinheads to publish their own magazines or maintain their own radio stations, for instance, but via electronic mail they can virtually do both on very limited funds. On the other hand, worthwhile groups could form as well. The family will face this dilemma both as a group and as individual members.

The new media world is simultaneously filled with more communication "choices" and fraught with potential cultural chaos. Unless we maintain strong local, low-tech communication, the superhighways can easily overwhelm the family. Only interpersonal, relational communication can provide enough personal stability to allow us to keep the electronic maze in perspective. This is why it is essential for families to balance their time among high-tech and low-tech media. We need to know where we stand—what we believe and value—before we travel on the electronic superhighways. Otherwise we might get lost on an obscure back road or get overwhelmed by all the traffic on the main thoroughfares.

Privacy issues. The new superhighways will turn privacy into a major public issue. On the one hand, they will make possible incredible invasions of personal and family privacy. The more communication we do through any centralized technological system, the easier it is for others to find out what we've been up to, either for the purpose of marketing to us or, worse yet, in order to get information that can be used against us. Imagine that all of your telephone calls, video rentals and periodical subscriptions were available to savvy computer hackers who could sell the information to the highest bidder or loan it to your potential employers or to journalists. Now add such information as medical records, credit history, travel schedules and even personal mail. This type of scenario is very troubling and not extremely far-fetched. For all of the greater choice available on the new electronic superhighways, there is the shadowy specter of ruinous threats to personal privacy—a real vision of George Orwell's *1984*.

There is another, less obvious aspect to the privacy dilemma, however, which will challenge every family. The superhighway makes it much easier for each of us to "commune" privately with a much greater range of people and products. Just as cable TV enabled families and individuals to bring home movies previously available only in public settings, the digital communications revolution gives greater private access to once-public messages as well as to new private messages. Culture that used to be available only outside of the home is increasingly provided to individuals *inside* the home.

Surely the temptation to privately try various electronic services will lead some people into uncharted media worlds. It is difficult or embarrassing to commit oneself in public to certain activities; it is far easier to sample such things privately. Will families have the courage to maintain their public standards of taste and decency when the electronic highway runs through their homes? Or will Christians succumb to personal addictions and sinful media use as long as they can do so in private? Human nature suggests the latter, except for the workings of grace.

Time pressures. Perhaps above all, the greatest threat resulting from the current communications revolution is even stronger challenges to existing leisure time. By delivering more media messages directly into the home, the digital technologies make it far easier and probably less expensive to consume prepackaged entertainment and information. People might stay home even more for leisure pursuits, but they will not likely be communicating with family and other loved ones. Instead, they will be sitting before the computer screen or TV set, listening to music or talk shows, reading video texts, electronically ordering merchandise or services, and so on.

A good analogy is the difference between reading a few magazines delivered by the mail carrier and browsing the periodical shelves of a library. The former represents the old transportation highway, where people decided what to purchase and adjusted their reading habits accordingly. In that media world few of us would subscribe to dozens of periodicals, partly because of cost and partly because of limited reading time. Now we are entering a very different media environment, where people are more likely to fill their leisure time rather haphazardly with bits and pieces of messages from many sources. We'll be able to scan all kinds of databases, indexes, reports, newspapers, wire services, advertisements, dramas, musical services and the like. We can even "respond" to some of these by sending messages to other readers or in some cases directly to the writers or producers themselves.

In other words, the electronic superhighway will not be only a pay-per-ride service with known destinations—although that will certainly be part of it. Rather, it will be more similar to existing cable TV, where viewers zap channels to while away idle time. With more products and greater variety, the new system will seduce users to trade even greater amounts of their family time for media time. High-tech communication will be an even bigger threat to low-tech relationships.

The Computer Connection

As the new media technologies merge on the electronic superhighway, the most important device is the home computer. Once the computer is connected to the TV set and wires or fiber optics, it becomes a communications center, regulating the flow of messages into and out of the home.

Families must master the home computer in the new media world. Already over 25 percent of households in the United States have at least one computer, although over half of Americans say they are uncomfortable with the new technology. Parents had better learn this technology, because, as a writer for *The New York Times* put it, the keyboard is becoming a "hangout for a computer-savvy generation" of youth.

Fortunately, most schools are teaching computer basics, but parents also need to understand how these technologies work. One of the best ways for this to happen is for families to play together some of the more educational computer games. When my wife and I decided about five years ago that we and our children should be learning more about computers, we purchased a used, inexpensive one on the advice of knowledgeable friends. Before we knew it, the kids were bringing home copies of public domain software (noncopyrighted material that can legally be copied) from friends. Soon the children were unbelievably fluent in these high-tech "languages." Fortunately, we had purchased the same type of computer system they and their friends were learning in school.

As the months went by, my wife and I learned how to play many of these games with the help of our offspring. We actually were beginning to incorporate the computer into family life, using it to bring us together for fun and discussion. The next step was to purchase some more sophisticated programs, both to increase our family pleasure and to enhance understanding of this new technological toy. We did that, but only gradually, in order to keep the computer within family life and to avoid producing our own "hackers"—computer wizards who spend voluminous amounts of time in front of their screens, often at the expense of personal relationships.

Finally, we purchased an upgraded computer and enough equipment to connect our house to the outside world. Now that we were all more or less computer literate, it was time to commune with people, places and organizations we knew very little about. A modem, which connects the computer to a telephone line or cable-TV wires, and a subscription to one of the major information services did the trick. Our daughter, who is highly social, wasn't especially interested in using the new equipment. Our teenage son, on the other hand, immediately started importing into our home all kinds of news, information, images and sounds. Interestingly enough, at first he was not keen about meeting new friends on the computer services. He felt more secure using the computer like an information-retrieval service, especially to retrieve computer games and special graphics created by unknown writers. As he became more comfortable with the technology, though, he began exploring person-to-person communication on the network. Needless to say, this worried us.

Based on his experience at school, our son rightly advised us that the computer was a good means of doing some types of educational activities. So we purchased a few inexpensive programs for his schoolwork, primarily programs that provided geographic and cultural data, lexicons and thesauruses. Meanwhile, he figured out how to do "library" research for his school papers partly via the on-line information services. All along he and his younger sister were teaching themselves keyboarding (formerly "typing"), word processing (formerly such things as setting tabs, adding page numbers and revising text), simple graphics (formerly impressing the teacher with cover-sheet drawings and illustrations) and printing (getting the material printed on the paper). No matter what area of work they eventually enter, the children will have learned valuable skills. By learning these things when they were young, our children likely avoided some of the anxiety (if not dysfunction) that accompanies adults' attempts to learn a new "language."

For all of these benefits, however, the danger is very real that some youth will become so enmeshed in the computer world that the electronic superhighway takes them on a joyride out of their own home. Kids need to learn much of the computer "language" on their own, with assistance from teachers and especially peers. But adults need to stay with their offspring for as much of the ride as is feasible. Too much parental involvement will likely hinder the child's creative potential in the new media, but too little may provide children with too much unstructured freedom—freedom to waste time or even to abuse it with unhealthy activities and associations.

As a college teacher, I've noticed a relationship between young adults' heavy media use, including the use of computers, and undeveloped social skills. In conversation with some of these students I discovered that their media affinity began long before high school, usually in the early adolescent years. While other children their age were beginning to exercise their social abilities, the media aficionados diverted more energy to "communing" with their favorite technologies. They were well connected to computers, but not so well to friends or sometimes even family.

For all these reasons, computers should be introduced enthusiastically into the home, but only if the parents are committed to integrating the new technology into family life. Christian young people need to be computer-savvy, because this marvel can also be the beast that introduces many decadent and sinful messages into our homes and the homes of our children. As I look into the future through the lens of current technological developments, I see computers sitting on the throne of power, regulating the electronic superhighway.

Wouldn't it be wonderful if the Christian youth of today were the wise and discerning traffic police on that highway of the future?

High-Tech Families

If Christian families can't opt out of the new media world, they can use it to their advantage. With the help of parents, children can learn to use the high-tech media to promote low-tech communication and God-glorifying relationships. The following guidelines are crucial for family life.

1. Add the new technologies to your family life slowly. Adding them quickly will increase family stress and make it very difficult to find a reasonable role for each technology in daily activities.

2. Prepare a general plan for using the new technology. When will it be used? For how much time? By whom? Where will it be located in the house? Why? Of course you'll probably change your minds about some things later. But without a plan, bad habits will likely set in, and once they're in place they'll be very hard to change.

3. Make the new technology a family affair right from the start. I'm always amazed at the number of parents who simply give VCRs or computers to their children, with no desire to be part of the child's technological life. It's almost as if the parents view the new gadgets as a toy instead of as a communications technology. The new electronic superhighway will shock a lot of parents even more than did "old-fashioned" radio and TV. Parents should take an interest in the new technology right from the beginning, learning as much as possible *with* the child.

4. As a family, regularly discuss the new technology. Don't let the technology drift off to a private place in the lives of one or more family members. Even if you don't use the technology very often, but your children do, raise the topic during moments of nonstressful quality time. Be as positive as possible: "What do you like about it?" "What programs or information services do you most enjoy?" "Why?" Then listen before responding. And avoid *any* critical comments until you've had a chance to look or listen to the material yourself. Even then, don't stop listening.

5. *Tell your own stories of technologies of the past.* This is a fabulous way to promote family understanding and discussion of new technologies. Our children have been fascinated to hear about the old floor-model radio we had in the basement of the house in which I grew up—the one that received even police calls and shortwave. They also have gotten a kick out of stories about 45-rpm records and top-40 radio stations, about the "party-line" telephone we had, about my first transistor radio—and how I listened to it at night under the pillow—about my brother's Cadillac radio mounted under the dash in his 1955 Dodge, the enormous radio with tubes and a mechanical "station-search" that was a precursor to today's "scan" features. By telling these stories, not only do we teach our children about our pasts but, just as important, we encourage them to tell *their* stories about today's technologies. We can expect to learn lessons about the technologies as we make our own parallels between the electronic highway and the coming superhighway.

The Global Metropolis

In a song about people and the new media, Bruce Springsteen tells us there were "57 Channels (and Nothin' On)." It's a common refrain in our media-saturated world—so much technology and so little worthwhile content. Surely this is one of the great ironies and one of the most telling facts of our culture.

Media guru Marshall McLuhan coined a misleading phrase that people love to use to describe the new media world: "the global village." While many technologies are increasingly global, neither people's access to them nor their content resembles anything like life in a village. Even with the BBCs and CNNs of the world, the globe is hardly a community, let alone a village. Instead we are witnessing the growth of a number of competing media empires, each creating a smorgasbord of entertainment and information for disparate audiences. Instead of an electronic village, we've got something like a global city with a myriad different ethnic groups, nationalities, religions, lifestyles and ideologies. This cultural variety is more starkly visible today than ever, and largely because of the new media technologies.

Whether we want it or not, our children are growing up in this new media world. It will be increasingly impossible for parents, pastors and teachers to isolate youth from the broader world. Certainly children need some protection. But most of all they need to learn Christianly about this media world as a kind of spiritual inoculation, so they can enter and transform the world for the kingdom of God. We do our offspring a disservice if we leave them naive about fax machines, cellular telephones, computers, cable and fiber optics, and anything else that comes down the digital superhighway. Instead we should make them wise for the tasks ahead so that they become what Bob Briner, an accomplished television producer, calls "roaring lambs" in his book of the same title.

The Muslim group opposed to satellite dishes in Kuwait probably overstated its case. We can't lay the blame for AIDS and herpes on the technology. But these religious people are at least taking a stand in support of their moral values and spiritual beliefs, whereas the optimistic homemaker seems to value little more than individual freedom and fun. She indeed represents the affluent West, where personal pleasures are often put ahead of society and even the family.

5
Home Improvement

Establishing Family Media Standards

One morning our daughter came home looking particularly tired after a sleepover with a few of her friends. We figured that she had been up much of the night, giggling, telling stories, playing games and engaging in other typical sleepover antics. But this time things were different. She was emotionally exhausted, not just physically tired. What was wrong?

Over the next half hour we discovered what had happened at the sleepover. Her host's parents had decided to show the girls a video. By adult standards it was not a bad movie, but its appropriateness for young audiences was questionable. Unthinkingly, they showed the film simply to amuse the kids. And the parents didn't view it with the girls, or even ask them in advance whether they should check with their parents. The hosts' intentions were admirable, but their lack of judgment dumbfounded us.

Our daughter suffered because of that poor judgment. She was emotionally drained and mentally confused by the movie's adult themes and situations. She spent a sleepless, frightening night instead of an enjoyable time with friends. In fact, for a number of months afterward our daughter was reluctant to accept any sleepover invitations unless we contacted the parents to see if any videos were going to be shown. This was a bit uncomfortable for us, since our inquiries could be interpreted as questioning the judgment of other parents. Even so, it was our parental responsibility. In the long run, this painful episode helped us better understand our daughter, ourselves and the world in which our children are growing up.

As the media world expands into an electronic superhighway, the need for family standards will be even greater. Each new technology tends to be used by the entertainment industry to broaden the scope of available products, both for good and for bad. Without standards, a family can't know where it stands, and every media decision is either a new struggle or a thoughtless decision. In most Christian homes, I believe, the latter is true. Children learn to be thoughtless by the example of their parents, who solve the media problem by giving each family member his or her own technology instead of by establishing common media standards.

Fred Rogers of *Mr. Rogers' Neighborhood* fame nicely summarized this situation: "[Kids don't] really know if the family approves or disapproves of what is on [TV]. All they know is that mother and father bought it, brought it in there and set it in the middle of the living room. And how are they to know that it really does or doesn't reflect the family tradition?" The same could be said for each of the media, from radio to computers and cable TV.

This chapter addresses the essential need for family standards, although my slant on this topic is more positive than the way the subject is typically addressed in Christian circles. As I will show, the task of setting media standards is not just a *problem,* but an *opportunity* for building spiritual discernment in the home. If parents approach this opportunity in the right way, the media can provide occasions for families to communicate and grow together spiritually.

In subsequent chapters I'll look at this opportunity from the perspective of younger children versus adolescents and teens. In this chapter, I'll set the scene for using the media productively in the service of family life and spiritual development.

What's a Standard?

I know from my experiences on the lecture circuit that the word *standard* means many different things to Christian parents. The most common view is that a standard is a *restriction.* A standard draws the line somewhere in the culture, making some activities or products acceptable and others unacceptable. For example, I hear repeatedly that certain movies are unacceptable because they are rated "R" or because they have too much violence. In other words, a standard is an easily understood yardstick that makes some media off limits and others, presumably, in bounds.

Although there is some wisdom in this approach, it leads to some major problems when children reach adolescence and begin looking for *reasons* for the restrictions. I've met many adolescents who cannot communicate well with their parents about the media because the standards they grew up with were all stated negatively as restrictions, without any positive rationale. Christian children often hear from parents a lot of no's about media that the children seem to enjoy. And without any reasons for the restrictions, such children will increasingly divorce their parents' "standards" from their own experience.

Real standards are *restrictions with positive reasons.* As parents, we often focus on the restriction without giving adequate thought to the benefit behind the restriction. The result is a missed opportunity for building communication between parents and children, as well as a missed chance to improve spiritual discernment as a family. By and large, our offspring want to know the *value* of a restriction—what they will *gain,* not just what they will lose. Obviously very young children cannot easily be reasoned with, and parents often have to establish standards for them. But even preschool children benefit from hearing a discussion of real standards: even if they don't completely understand the reasons, it teaches them implicitly that reasons are important. Yet a recent study in the *Journal of Broadcasting & Electronic Media* found that even though preschoolers' access to VCRs is considerable, parental rules for use of the technology are "often unspoken and invoked arbitrarily."

In addition, when standards include positive reasons, they can encourage all family members to participate in the process of building discernment. I'll never forget the time my five-year-old son walked into the family room while I was watching the evening news. He looked at the tube, turned directly to me and hit me with this question: "Dad, are you watching the news again?"

Immediately I thought to myself, *Yes I am, you little stinker! What business is it of yours?* I bit my tongue and replied calmly, "Yes, son. Why do you ask?"

"Well," he began slowly, "you shouldn't watch the news because it makes you grouchy."

In one simple sentence my son had caught me cold. The more I thought about it, the more I recognized that he was right. TV news *did* often put me in a bad mood, both because of the tomfoolery in the reporting and because of the actual subjects covered in the reports. Newspapers didn't bother me much, but TV news did. I couldn't sit calmly in front of the tube and have high-paid, freshly coiffured reporters tell "the truth." Their arrogance and sometimes their ignorance riled me. My son felt this, even if he didn't fully understand it. He realized that it was better for the family if Dad was in a good mood. Either I would have to change my viewing response or I would have to give up TV news. I did the latter—and at the request of a little kid!

Similarly, a few years back my family got into a major discussion at the dinner table about whether Christians should listen to "non-Christian" music. The subject was launched by one of our children, who was deeply into the contemporary Christian music scene at the time. Before long we were cordially embroiled in a debate about what "Christian art" really is, from music to movies to novels. As long as we argued only about whether it was acceptable to listen to the local rock radio stations, we didn't get very far. Once we expanded the discussion, we had a real opportunity for building common understanding.

Eventually we agreed that there are no easy definitions of "Christian art," but that we should always seek art that would please God because of its beauty, purity, truthfulness and so on (Philippians 4:8). We now had a standard that was biblical and that included a powerful and positive reason, not just a humanly created restriction. Moreover, we had a standard that was so widely applicable that we could come back to it again and again for family discussion.

Focusing on the Big Issues

When I was a new father, a colleague gave me some of the best parenting advice I've ever received: "Focus on what's really important, and give your kids some freedom to make mistakes in areas that are less important. In other words, pick your battles very carefully." The "battle" image troubled me, but the overall advice was so sound and so practical that I've never forgotten it. Years later I realized how important this advice is for building media discernment.

Many parents err by focusing their standards on relatively unimportant issues. This happens all the time with parental reactions to MTV, the music television channel aimed at adolescents. Parents tune it in for a few minutes and immediately go bonkers over the wild clothing and hairstyles of the artists and program hosts. I must admit that I myself don't like the kind of bohemian dress favored on the channel. But the cultural clash between MTV and "genteel" suburbia is not primarily a sartorial issue, is it?

In making our judgments about MTV or other media worlds, we have to press for the big issues. If MTV's program is countercultural or even just some sexually provocative clothing, the channel may not be very bad relative to other media. But the clothing reflects a deeper reality, a kind of anarchistic and hedonistic attitude toward life. The fundamental problem is not that MTV challenges middle-class values, which also deserve criticism in light of the gospel. Rather, MTV is like Solomon's search for earthly pleasure, where nothing is denied the self but where everything in the end turns out to be "a chasing after the wind" (Ecclesiastes 2:11).

The truth is that MTV repeatedly affirms selfish pleasure as a philosophy of life: buy what *you* want, have sex with whom *you* want, wear what *you* want, enjoy whatever *you* want, criticize those whom *you* want to criticize. This pervasive philosophy on MTV is a very big issue because it contradicts directly the selfless love of the gospel. For this reason, much of MTV is very bad stuff that turns us away from the good and focuses on evil.

I'm repeatedly confounded by the ways that parents zero in on relatively unimportant issues and virtually miss the big ones. I hear about the "beat" of the music on one radio station, about a provocative scene in a forthcoming TV show, about the rating of a current movie, about the language in a school novel. But rarely do I hear parents talking about the overall worldview or fundamental values of these works of popular art. I have to conclude that our evaluation of these products is rather superficial and based on "quick-and-dirty" criteria rather than spiritual wisdom.

The most important consideration is the "heart" behind the message, and we can't get at that heart without listening and looking for it. Suppose my daughter wants to listen regularly to a local rap-music station. My initial reaction is very unfavorable, largely because I don't like the rap music I've heard and because I don't trust the people who are making it. After all, I've heard a few reports that rap music is sexually suggestive, perhaps even obscene. Moreover, in my mind rap music is connected to the ghetto, the drug culture, urban violence, pregnant teens and broken families. Based on all this "information," I tell my daughter that she can't listen to the rap station.

A few days later she hands me a tape by a so-called Christian rap group. Now what do I do? Suddenly my assumptions about the music are called into question. I wonder if rap music per se is the issue— or is it the heart behind the music? Then I take the bold step of listening to the recording with my daughter. I still don't like the music, but the lyrics are remarkably biblical, and they directly challenge my stereotypes. Now I'm forced into looking at the bigger issues, and I have to reconsider my own cultural standards in light of the gospel.

This process of trying to get to the root of discernment is both exciting and frustrating. It's exciting for families because root issues force us to deal openly with basic spiritual matters rather than relying on our personal taste, cultural arrogance or stereotypes. And it brings parents and children together in the process. It's frustrating, however, because often things are not so black-and-white once we start trying to get at the deeper issues. When our neat and cozy categories are challenged, we might fear that we'll have no standards left or that we'll become too liberal and wishy-washy.

By focusing on the minor issues rather than the major ones, we often slip into simplistic or misguided standards that are a disservice to our own quest for spiritual wisdom and godly lives. Usually minor issues create rigid standards because the rationale is weak. When such rigidity breaks, there can be worse chaos than there would be from open exploration of the big issues.

Once after giving a public presentation on MTV to hundreds of teens, I found myself counseling a long line of disgruntled youth. Oddly enough, they generally agreed with my argument that most MTV was not worth watching because of its nihilistic, carnal, selfish view of life. They were upset, however, that their parents had hastily rejected the video channel without considering the fact that not all rock videos are evil. Their parents' oversimplification of the situation reduced the teens' trust in parental judgment about all media and culture.

Three Pitfalls
Even parents who strive for the best standards should beware of three major pitfalls.

1. Hypocrisy. If parents think this is a minor problem, they ought to reconsider. One of the biggest refrains I hear from adolescents is "My parents' media are just as bad," or "What about my mom's novels or my dad's movies?" Some savvy youth even go further, pointing out the violence in Sunday-afternoon football, the materialism in commercials or the female idolatry in women's magazines. I've heard college students remark about the "junk novels" their parents read—the same parents who criticized their kids during high school for watching "TV trash."

Most of this hypocrisy seems to stem from a false notion that adults need not be as concerned with standards for themselves as they are with standards for their children. Having become adults, so the argument goes, parents are free to decide for themselves which media are worthwhile and which are worthless. While maturity certainly carries with it some privileges, such as the option to view movies or read books with adult themes, it shouldn't mean limitless media use or thoughtless consumption.

Children quickly pick up on parents' attitudes as they are reflected in actual behavior. Unless parents show by example that adult privileges entail applying adult standards, their hypocrisy will breed spiritual immaturity among their children. As long as adulthood symbolizes unbridled freedom, children will see restrictive parents as hypocrites.

Parents lead not only by what they say to their children but by what they actually do. Therefore, they should be leaders by example in love (1 John 4:7-16). When children see parents examining their own media choices and grappling with the tough issues, the children learn that standards are a worthwhile and lifelong process. Even if the children don't adopt precisely the parents' standards, they will likely seek meaningful standards of their own instead of mere personal satisfaction.

2. Deception. Parental deception will also hinder the possibility of establishing common family standards. The most typical form of deception is pretending to know more about particular media products or their effects than we really do. In order to persuade the children to adopt particular standards, parents seize hold of any statement that seems to support their preexisting standards.

This kind of deception is not the result of evil intent, but comes about because of parents' need to justify their standards. Sometimes parents will pick up on a story in the popular media about the alleged effects of particular TV programming or musical lyrics. Other times they'll take sides in an ongoing public debate about the media, using media quotes to buttress their position. Still other times parents simply seize upon a public rumor or existing commonplaces about the media. For decades many parents assumed, for instance, that viewing TV in a darkened room would cause vision problems, but there was never really any evidence to support this contention. In fact, studies have shown that such viewing apparently has no negative effects.

Honesty would suggest that we carefully consider whether there is really any basis for the standards we wish to share with our children. Are we acting out of fear and ignorance, or do we have evidence to claim that our views of the media are trustworthy? Are we just looking for information that confirms our preconceptions, or are we really open to the possibility that we could be wrong? Once again, we risk losing our children's trust if we pretend to know much more with certainty than we really do.

It is especially important that we have at least some experience with the media enjoyed by our children. We can't legitimately claim to know about these media, and to make judgments about them, without having read, listened to or viewed them, preferably with the children. We must try to understand what the medium means in their lives— why they like it and why they want to commit their time to it instead of to other media.

For several years my daughter was deeply involved with her friends in reading a large series of contemporary fiction books about the adventures of a small group of baby-sitting adolescents. In fact, the books were so popular that the publisher had to have been using ghost writers to meet the rising demand. Often my daughter discovered inconsistencies of plot and character in the series. Nevertheless, she loved these popular novels and voraciously read them, sometimes more than one per day. The kids' school librarian and I, both lovers of "great" fiction, were chagrined by this invasion of second-rate tales. My wife and I delicately suggested other books to my daughter during that time, but with little success.

Then two things happened that changed our limited, elitist view of matters. First, my daughter began baby-sitting. Suddenly we realized how important this activity was for her developing self-confidence and self-esteem. To her, baby-sitting symbolized the move into adulthood, and without any younger brothers or sisters she had previously had no one to care for other than the family dog. Part of the lure of those novels had been their peek into this adult world of real responsibilities.

Second, during this period we also first recognized how crucial our daughter's peer relationships were to her. She was beginning to derive much encouragement and support from her more trustworthy peers—the ones she could open up with and "commune" with at sleepovers and school breaks. The novels fit into that overall need for peer relationships, partly because the stories dealt with close adolescent friendships and partly because our daughter and her close friends used the books to generate discussion about their own relationships. In other words, the fiction provided a common body of stories for her and her friends to discuss real life.

My ignorance of the importance of these books in her life had made it easy for me to be critical. Without taking the time to empathize with my daughter, I had been far too simplistic and self-serving. My concern was certainly legitimate, but my deceptively ignorant standard—good literature versus bad literature—was of little value to my daughter. Fortunately, I never pushed the issue of these novels, for if I had done so I might have created some real communication problems in the family. Parents make this type of mistake with many media, from soap operas to teen flicks and girls' magazines. Without empathy, our knowledge of these media is invariably shallow, and our criticisms, no matter how well intentioned, are frequently deceptive.

My wife, by contrast, went so far as to read some of the books our daughter so enjoyed. She was then able to talk with her about the stories and the social issues they addressed. Our daughter, in turn, was gratified to know that Mom cared about what *she* cared about. While my opinions of the novels were based deceptively on very little real information, my wife's knowledge of them came from actual experience and genuine mother-daughter discussion. In that context, our daughter was much more likely to heed her mother's discernment than her father's attitude.

3. Stubbornness. Once we take a position, it is not always easy to change our point of view. We dig in like infantry in foxholes on the front lines of a war, firing salvos and holding on to our helmets when volleys are returned. We don't want to give up any ground we have "won" previously through hard work or luck. Especially with adolescents, we often resent being challenged and become more and more inflexible over time.

Of course there are big issues that we probably ought not to negotiate—the basic issues of identity and godliness. But a totally inflexible parent, with no room for negotiation or revision, sends the wrong message to offspring. Stubbornness signals that children don't really matter, and it can elicit stubborn responses that destroy communication.

Media standards need to be negotiated, not mandated. Again, this is less possible with younger children than with adolescents, but it is a very important consideration for avoiding "exasperated" offspring (Ephesians 6:4). Stubbornness implicitly says that we have no time for our children or that we don't care about their feelings. We can be principled—committed to particular standards—without being inflexible and close-minded. Indeed, children can learn much from principled parents, while stubborn parents generally irritate and frustrate offspring.

Stubbornness is especially damaging in the area of media standards because of the amount of generational segregation and the dynamic nature of the media. Few adults have the time to bridge the generational gap by consuming youth-oriented media alongside their offspring. So parents are bound to misunderstand some youth media and to make some mistakes about what music or television or movies are acceptable.

We need to be flexible enough to revise our views and change how we apply our standards. With the media changing so rapidly, we would be foolhardy not to remain open-minded. An R-rated film of yesterday could be equivalent to a PG-13 movie today. A new teen-oriented series on the Fox network could embrace better values than those of earlier series. The rap music on one radio station might not be like the rap on another one. A recently released video game could be far more educational and less addictive than the last one we bought.

The most damaging kind of stubbornness, however, stems from the mistaken belief that the media of one's own era were better than those of any later time. It seems that every generation of adults partly falls into this trap by assuming that movies have gone downhill, that today's TV is for the birds, that music used to be better, that newspapers now focus only on negative news or have gone liberal, that contemporary fiction is trash; therefore, the solution to today's media problems is to criticize the contemporary stuff and hold up the old stuff as a better example.

Frankly, this kind of media romanticism never quite works. People want to hold up *Leave It to Beaver* as an example of great family fare, but they forget about the vaudevillian comedy of the same era, from Milton Berle to Jerry Lester, or about *The Honeymooners* and *The Naked City*. Other parents point back to great show tunes of the 1950s and 1960s, but they ignore the popular music laced with assumptions of sexual promiscuity—some of it sung by Frank Sinatra and Tony Bennett, not just top-40 artists. Similarly, adults will fondly recall movie "classics" such as *The Sound of Music* without remembering *Midnight Cowboy* or *The Graduate*. Especially in the United States, nostalgia is a kind of national sickness that impairs people's ability to reason about history.

I'm not saying that media have gotten better, just that nostalgic stubbornness will not help parents establish common family standards for the contemporary media. Parents' past taste in media is hardly adequate for today's world of cable TV, international satellites and compact discs. In fact, what we enjoyed as children was probably criticized by our parents. It doesn't always make sense to hold up those older products as symbols of a better era, more refined taste or moral purity.

Media Events

Perhaps the most helpful means of bringing the family together for establishing common standards is the "media event." As I suggested in chapter two, for too many families the media have become little more than means for individual members to occupy their leisure time. Families do very little collective media use, preferring instead to seek personal diversions in a book, periodical, computer game, TV show and the like. This type of individualistic response to the media world makes it nearly impossible for families to find a communal identity rooted in shared standards of culture.

The families that have the best handle on viewing standards often differ from others in one crucial respect: they set aside time together for special media activities. We discovered the value of this approach to family media use when we purchased our first VCR. This technology forced us to talk together about which tapes we were going to rent, why we should rent them, how each of us felt about different films and, most important, what criteria we would use to decide which tapes to rent. It was a very different process from merely going our own ways, each to his or her own technology and media content. Later, when the children were adolescent, we discovered that the same procedure worked well for moviegoing, evening television, auto-trip tape recordings and the like.

Here's how the "media event" works: A family decides in advance when it will spend media-related leisure time together. Normally this will be in the evening, most often on the weekend. Let's say that Saturday evenings are reserved by the entire clan for media use. A few days in advance, family members discuss during dinner how they would like to spend the upcoming evening. A quick review of the local arts paper reveals a host of interesting options, including civic and professional theater, first-run movies, concerts and sports events. In addition there are the "old standbys," including television, videotapes, and video and computer games. The newspaper probably lists new video releases, although a quick call to the local video shop would probably be even more helpful. Not all of these options are mass media events, but they're all cultural events, broadly speaking.

Now how will you decide together which special "event" to enjoy? You'll want to discuss your individual preferences, of course, but you'll also have to strive for some type of unanimity or compromise. If your family includes younger and older children, this could be a real challenge. And how will you feel if the children's preferences are considerably different from your own? When children are young, their parents are often willing to sacrifice their "own" free time for a day at the zoo or some other activity with the youngsters. But as the children grow up, there is a strong, selfish desire to let them do their own thing so the parents can do theirs as well.

Media-event planning appropriately forces the family to be more aware of its own implicit standards. The entire family has to communicate, revealing individual preferences and values. Moreover, selfish motives become abundantly clear, as do peer influences ("All of my friends have already seen it"), expert opinions ("The paper gave it a great review") and hearsay ("I heard it's a bomb"). Suddenly everyone's opinions and their sources are open to family scrutiny. In our home this type of discussion has become so commonplace that members prepare for it by reading reviews, talking to friends and organizing their arguments for the most persuasive impact. Family discussions are laced with biblical references and theological ideas— even from the kids.

Family media events also provide an opportunity for post-event reflection together. Normally we're barely out of the door of a theater or have just stopped the VCR when someone offers the first insightful critique, such as "Fabulous flick," "It stunk," "There was almost no plot," "I really liked it," "Terrible acting" or "What a bunch of foul language!"

After out-of-home media events, we usually head to a restaurant for dessert and discussion. There we sit, face to face, talking not only about the event itself but also about the pre-event discussion. We take turns basking in the glory of our well-selected activity or tactfully placing egg on the appropriate person's face—all in good fun, of course. My wife and I have discovered to our amazement that the children are often harsher critics than we are. Also, when all the give-and-take discussion is over, they're the ones most likely to learn immediately from the experience and to put it into practice for the next pre-event discussion.

We've discovered, then, that the media-event approach to planned leisure makes our family life more fun and more mutually instructive. It lifts entertainment from the individualist realm of personal taste and makes the media part of our shared lives and our common quest for standards. It keeps both the kids and the parents on their cultural toes. Finally, it reminds my wife and me to be good listeners and to value our kids' contributions. Very likely this helps boost the children's self-esteem as well, as they discover that their hearts and minds truly matter in the family.

The only major drawback to this approach, in our estimation, is that sometimes we get burned on a particularly poor, offensive or inappropriate activity. Even when we do our homework, such as soliciting opinions from friends and relying on generally trusted critics, there is still the possibility that we made a poor judgment. We have found ourselves turning off the VCR in the middle of a movie. But isn't this a risk no matter what we do with the media—unless we put our heads in the sand and turn off *all* technology, including books and magazines?

At least the media-event approach gives the parents and children an opportunity to discuss the bad as well as the good, all with the motive of bringing godly discernment and appreciation to bear on the surrounding culture. In our view, it's well worth the extra effort, because this approach turns the biggest family problem with the media—the destruction of interpersonal communication—on its head. We use the

media to generate conversation and enhance relationships in the
family.

Freedom and Responsibility

Someone once described the Christian life to me as an unusual com-
bination of freedoms and responsibilities existing side by side in
healthy tension. Certainly there's a lot more to being a Christian, but
our day-to-day lives are indeed filled with the struggle to live respon-
sibly in the freedom granted to us by Christ. Modern culture is so
loaded with opportunities to make choices that we sometimes forget
about our responsibility to live in ways pleasing to God. On the other
hand, we can take responsibility so seriously that we never exercise
the freedom to unwittingly err and thereby to grow and mature in
Christ. Parenting in a media world is nothing less than the task of
managing cultural freedom so our families don't drown in it, while
encouraging responsibility for our offspring and ourselves.

Mr. Rogers nicely summarized the responsibility of parents this
way: "The parent should be a parent, caretaker, someone who provides structure, confidence, and safety." Within this responsibility, parents have to provide enough freedom for children to exercise their
creative gifts, including the gift of critical discernment. As this gift is
developed, a child can begin to live a truly holy life informed by
spiritual wisdom and distinguishable from the ways of the world.

Parents who lord it over their children, afraid of every cultural
challenge and unable to provide any room for them to make mistakes,
have traded all freedom for the false security of perfect responsibility.
Eventually the child who grows up in a media-deprived world will
have to face the real world on his or her own, without parental guid-
ance.

Sometimes I see this even at college, where students who were raised without having to make their own media choices are suddenly confronted with so much freedom that they cannot cope with it. Either they break loose from the past, lurching into cultural promiscuity, or they tend to pull back even further into the comfort of the past. These latter young adults occasionally become reactionary critics of the media who can find no good in the products that their more liberal peers thoroughly enjoy. They are like aliens in their own generation.

On the other end of the spectrum are the children raised with so much freedom that they view any discernment as merely outdated regulations imposed by people who don't know how to have fun. Like the group that doesn't want freedom, these youth are largely the product of their upbringing. For them, technology is merely a playground, not a vehicle for taking care of and developing God's creation. Their parents have squelched the communication between God and their offspring, so that only the horizontal dimension of life, the cultural here and now, carries any moral weight. And that morality is not responsibility as much as peer pressure or self-fulfillment. The cultural compass of such young people spins around wildly with every change of fad and fashion in music, video, film and the other media.

Our children need a vigorous cultural life that balances freedom and responsibility for the kingdom of God. Parents are in the best position to make this happen, and they should avoid the temptation to turn the job over to schools or churches, which can support but never replace the family. Normally no one is more important in a child's life than the parents. My father, a man who endured many heartaches and enjoyed few material blessings, somehow knew this intuitively even though he was never deeply religious. He muddled through the job of parenting, rarely sure of the exact road to take, but nevertheless a mentor for integrity and conviction. We may make a lot of mistakes as we try to balance freedom and responsibility with our children, but our conviction to do so will often say more to them than any actual success we might have at doing it.

Four Media Idols of Our Age

In the contemporary media world there are four recurring values that seriously challenge the Christian faith. We would be remiss as parents if we did not address them in our discussions with our children.

1. Consumerism. In Western cultures, especially the United States, the love of "stuff" is so pervasive that it's hard to see its cultural power in our own lives. Commercials, movies, prime-time TV and the whole celebrity system in the entertainment industry are founts of the consumerist mentality. Once our identity is tied to what we can buy and display, this ethic has successfully invaded our lives. We need to embrace the goodness of the material world without succumbing to any kind of material idolatry, the great sin of greed.

2. Secular evil. The media world has very little room for sin. It has replaced sin with a kind of secular evil disconnected from God. There are plenty of good and bad figures in the media world, including on the news and in video games, but there is no eternal reference point for identifying transgressions against God. Even some of the most despicable movies have a certain sense of right and wrong, but their universe is typically too small for sin. May our children hear from us, over and over again, that evil is only a manifestation of a much deeper human problem that demands a Savior.

3. Individualism. Today's media often appeal to humankind's most rudimentary sense of selfishness: each of us is in the world primarily to serve ourselves, to maximize personal pleasure and to follow our own path to freedom. We see this in the undue emphasis on individual sports champions, the individual heroes who pervade Westerns and detective shows, the individual bodies paraded in advertisements and so on across the spectrum of popular culture. Christianity responds to this with a call for selfless living and a commitment to the community of believers. None of us is an island.

4. External beauty. Thanks largely to the pervasive growth of the image-making media—magazines, movies, TV, billboards—the human body has become one of the major icons of our time. In chapter seven I will address this in the context of the teenage years, when identities are especially fragile. But across the years of human life, external "beauty" is defined and elevated by the media to a degree that reveals cultural sickness. Everyone evaluates their worth more or less by this antibiblical standard. The Scriptures, by contrast, hold up the internals of the human heart for evaluation. We would truly have a different culture if we examined our hearts instead of our body shape, skin complexion and apparel.

In but Not of the Media World

In a media world, where the family is adrift in a sea of technologies and messages, Christians must be as wise as serpents about the surrounding culture. It is simply not possible to close the hatch and submerge the family like a cultural submarine. Even if we turned off all of the media, our children would be influenced by peers, neighbors, other relatives and friends who still used the technologies. Unless we decide to become total cultural hermits, we must live in this media world.

Our task is to remain in this world without conforming to it, without being *of* the world. Creating an understanding of the difference between living *in* and *of* the media world is one of the central tasks of parenting. We do this through our example—living by standards—and also by testing the cultural waters with and for our children, by subjecting the media spirits of the age to the light of the gospel. In this chapter I've asked parents to do this in love as a service to both Christ and their offspring.

When our daughter returned from her sleepover, emotionally shaken and fearful of the future, we saw anew how important parents are in the Christian home. We listened to her story. We empathized from our own childhood experiences. We gave encouragement and support so this small image-bearer of God would see and feel that the future is in God's hands. Finally, we helped her to see the popular idols of the day while inspiring her to value a godly life.

6

Growing Pains

Nurturing Kids in Medialand

I was working on a household project and needed some supplies. Always looking for a chance to spend some time with my first-grade son, I invited him along to the home-improvement section of a large retailer. We parked the car and hurried through the automatic doors, my young son half jogging to keep up with my long-legged pace. Once inside, we were hit with all of the "acceptable" sins of the day—lottery tickets on the left, booze on the right, and then display cases loaded with fresh-baked chocolate-covered donuts, apple fritters and fudge brownies. None of these temptations came even close to the big one we were about to face.

We wended our way down the center aisle of this superstore, dodging carts and snail-slow customers, on our way to the plumbing department. Suddenly my son stopped me dead in my tracks: "Dad! Hold up!"

I stopped, turned around and focused on my only son, who was kneeling before a large clearance bin marked "²/₃ off." I had seen these wire boxes before, having often rummaged through one to relieve boredom while my wife was carefully executing one or another great deal. They are usually filled with odds and ends, partial sets, unpackaged and damaged merchandise—all the junk that can be peddled only with a big "clearance" sign in a high-traffic area. In Dutch West Michigan, those signs are like a siren call.

I slowly walked back to my nearly prostrate son, who by this time was pleading with me to buy his fabulous find. "Dad, can I *please* have it? I've *always* wanted one," he said in the petitionary tones of a first-grader.

"What is it?" I asked with genuine curiosity.

"Dad," he said proudly, "it's He-Man underpants!"

I was flabbergasted. He-Man underpants? My son needed those like I needed Blues Brothers sunglasses or silk briefs for Valentine's Day.

But they *were* on clearance, and I wasn't up for a fight. And I did love my only son. So we got 'em. Such a deal!

Fifteen minutes later we were back home. We walked in the side door and my son shot like a bullet upstairs to his bedroom. Within seconds he was flying back downstairs and running at full speed around "the loop"—living room, dining room, kitchen—in endless cycles. I stood at the side door in disbelief, watching him make each round at seemingly faster speed, with his arms high in the air and adorned with nothing but the He-Man underpants.

For the first time I inspected the new apparel. The white briefs were very small, with a bright red elastic band around the top. On the front, in full color, was the animated He-Man himself, television's "master of the universe." On the back of the briefs was Skeletor, the show's villain. What marketing genius!

During the next few months my wife and I battled our son over whether he could wear those underpants every day. Instead of putting them in the wash each night, he would hide them under the bed or in a drawer in hopes of decorating his young body with the same superhero the next morning. Finally, in a fit of frustration, I confronted him: "Stephen, you can't wear those underpants every day!"

I'll never forget his response, which taught me one of the best lessons about parenting young kids in a media world: "But Dad, I have to! When I put them on, I feel like He-Man!"

Role Models for Morality

Of all of the points I could make about the importance of the media in the lives of preschoolers and early school-age children, none is more important than the power of media characters to become role models. Young children naturally seek heroic role models—generally older people to imitate, to look up to and to emulate. In a media world, which brings kids into contact with all kinds of people outside of home, church and school, media celebrities often serve as role models. This used to be true for books and fairy tales, and later for radio drama. Now it's especially true for movies and television, which make potential role models even more realistic. Parents, especially absent parents, can hardly compete with Saturday-morning TV and movie-action heroes.

The urge among kids to claim role models is especially powerful in the story media. Children want a clear sense that there is right and wrong in the world, and they gravitate to tales of moral certainty. These stories must provide heroes and villains, good guys and bad guys, who make this unambiguous moral universe come to life. For this reason the media are packed with moralistic stories for kids. We get Mighty Mouse, G.I. Joe, Ninja Turtles and Superman. It's good marketing, if not good storytelling as well.

Now we see more and more toys based on media heroes. In 1992 the Nickelodeon cable-TV channel and Mattel codeveloped a line of "activity toys" aimed at kids two to eleven years old. They knew what they were doing, because as the electronic media expand there is little difference between the entertainment industry and the toy business. The stories of one are driving the sales of the other, and vice versa.

By adding entertaining stories to the media mix, the marketers of role models can wield remarkable influence over the lives of young children. Today's toy stores are already loaded with media-related products, primarily from TV and movies. Each of these items represents not just corporate profits but, more important, a means of shaping the creative imagination of children. Kids use the toy characters, pajamas, underpants, lunch boxes and everything else to incorporate the media world into their imaginative play life. In other words, the media's moral universe becomes more or less their own as the children act out the kinds of morality plays programmed on television or in other media. These media are not primarily entertainers, but parentlike moral teachers.

In the early 1990s the television industry in the United States presumably admitted this, however unwittingly, in its response to the "Children's Television Act." According to the act, stations had to provide children with educational as well as entertaining programs. When it came time to document which shows met this requirement, stations responded by citing series like *The Jetsons, G.I. Joe, Leave It to Beaver* and *Super Mario Brothers.* The only reasonable conclusion is that virtually all programs are educational because they more or less teach children.

Media Versus Parents

From the time that youngsters begin watching TV and listening to audiotapes or radio, the media implicitly compete with parents as authority figures and moral teachers. This fact is generally overlooked or misunderstood by parents, who tend to see children's media through adult minds. Of course the media can support as well as challenge the values and beliefs that parents would like to teach their children. But few parents are adequately aware of when and how the media instruct their offspring, so they simply don't ask the hard questions with forethought and empathy. So let's take a look here at some of the major questions.

1. When are the media appropriate for kids? Generally speaking, all of the media are potentially appropriate when the child is developmentally ready. For example, parents can read to and play audiotapes for the child of about eighteen months to two years of age, as soon as the child shows enough interest and attention. Television might be appropriate at about three or four years of age, followed by children's own reading of books and periodicals. Finally, children of early school age are usually ready for interactive media, including computers and slower-paced video games.

The key to any use of the media in the home is *parental involvement.* All media are a considerable risk for little ones who are left on their own to interpret and respond to programs. Unless parents help children understand how the "outside" media world fits into their family activities, values and beliefs, children can come to all kinds of frightening and emotionally disturbing conclusions—even with media prepared carefully for youngsters by people who truly want to serve them.

Until about the age of eight, children are really not developmentally able to deal with the media without major parental assistance. At about this age children begin distinguishing between the media and "reality." In other words, not until about second or third grade is it really possible for children to begin to understand the difference between a make-believe world and their own day-to-day life. This includes the ability to understand the message or theme of a story they read, hear or see in the moving-image media. Prior to this time stories to them are "events"—people doing things—not ways of communicating about those events or, more broadly, about life.

Parents who use the media for baby-sitting typically are making a big mistake unless they have previewed the media and continuously talk about the media with their children. When we invite these media into our homes, we let them help raise the children. Fred Rogers put it bluntly: "Television is really part of the extended family now in people's homes. It's right in the living room." Warns Bob Keeshan of *Captain Kangaroo* fame, "Ninety-nine percent of parents don't care what their children watch on television because the parents use it as a babysitter." If Rogers and Keeshan are correct, as I believe, we fool ourselves if we think the tube and other media are "only entertainment" for kids.

Early in our parenting my wife and I took this problem very seriously. We decided to locate our only television at one end of the family room where it could also be seen in the living room, kitchen and dining area. This assured us that we would know what was on the set, so that we could discuss it with the children. The vast majority of our waking time was spent in one of those rooms; we would leave them only to answer the doorbell, run laundry upstairs and so forth. Frequently we would do our chores next to where our child was viewing the set, thereby both making ourselves available for discussion and monitoring the child's apparent responses to each show.

A study by the Gallup organization turned up some interesting support for this practice. It found that if parents felt uncomfortable about something they were viewing on television with their children, only 11 percent would explain the situation to their offspring. Almost half of the parents said they would switch the channel, and another 24 percent would just turn off the set, presumably to "protect" the children but certainly not helping them to understand the standard behind the decision. Only 4 percent would even express their disapproval to the children, let alone explain it. Interestingly, 8 percent said either they wouldn't do anything or they were unsure how they would respond.

What makes these data compelling is the fact that parents could assent to more than one of the responses to the question. In other words, they *could* have said they would discuss with the kids the reason for their discomfort *and* shut the set off, switch channels or whatever. Clearly, parents would rather ignore media problems or pretend they don't have to deal with them than use the problem as an opportunity for discussion and building discernment.

So the crucial question for parents is this: Are you willing to invest the time in helping your child understand a medium? If not, that medium is probably not yet appropriate in your household. High-tech media need a low-tech parent to supervise, interpret and monitor for trouble.

2. How are kids affected by the various media? The answer to this question depends on three major things: (1) the personality of the child, (2) the family context and (3) the actual content of the media. Frequently we parents focus on one or maybe two of these and overlook the others. In my judgment, parents often consider media content without paying adequate attention to the child's particular personality and to the overall family setting.

We know that not all children are influenced in the same ways by equivalent media content. Some children are extremely susceptible to the effects of TV violence or to the frenetic pace of video games. Even within the same family, two children can vary widely in the level of aggressive responses to violence. Similarly, some kids get virtually addicted to video games much more easily than others. It's not always easy to determine whether these differences are genetically tied to personality or created at least partly by various environmental variations, such as only-child status, parental modeling, even income and educational differences.

It is essential for parents to get to know each child as a "special" human being—to use Mr. Rogers's word. Talk matter-of-factly with each one about their feelings during and in response to various media content. Do the media seem to be emotionally powerful to them? Do they always seem to want more media stimulation? Are they able to move easily from the media to interpersonal communication and play? Do they bring up various media during quiet times, such as before naps or at bedtime? These sorts of questions are essential for monitoring the actual influence of a medium on your child.

When it comes to movies and TV with adult themes and situations, however, the general rule should be to protect young children by greatly limiting their access to these stories. It is irresponsible to permit a child's undeveloped emotional "equipment" to be bombarded by violent scenes and sexual situations, for instance, no matter how good the message of the show seems to be for adults. Kids are easily disturbed and confused by tales that they can't fit into their own life experiences. Our adult viewing standards won't work for our children. When we are in doubt, the simple rule should be "Turn it off."

School performance is indeed related to a child's media consumption, but not in an absolute way that makes it easy for parents to make the right decision with every child. For example, heavy TV viewing is usually associated with lower school grades, but not in every case.

Some very good students watch abundant TV, although often not the same shows as the lower-achieving children who view a lot. As a general rule, electronic media use interferes with schoolwork and with other activities that are crucial for classroom success, especially reading. Therefore, electronic media use should be balanced with reading periods.

Moreover, since the amount of reading a child will do drops off considerably during adolescence, it is crucial that parents encourage reading during earlier years. Nine-year-olds, for instance, are twice as likely as seventeen-year-olds to read books, according to a study by the American Federation of Teachers and the Chrysler Corporation. As the peer group becomes increasingly important during adolescence, solitary activities such as reading tend to lose their appeal for many young people.

3. Are particular TV programs usually better than others? All other things being equal, the answer is yes. My rule of thumb is simple but remarkably helpful: The faster the visual pace of the program, the worse the show for your children. Glitzy, fast-paced shows are very manipulative. In fact, commercials have the fastest pace on the tube, followed by rock videos and some animated programs. These programs will hold a child's attention often better than slower-paced ones, but children will not be better served.

Imagine a spectrum of programs, with animated action shows (*He-Man,* again) on one end, and slow-paced "educational" programs on the other end. A show like *Mr. Rogers' Neighborhood* is among the best for little kids because it is perhaps the slowest in all of videoland. Instead of trying to hook the children with visual stimulation, Rogers slowly develops each program's theme, carefully moves in and out of the land of make believe and ever so delicately talks with the little viewers. He calls it a "childlike" tempo. By comparison, many kids'

shows barrage viewers with mesmerizing images and abruptly changing sound effects. The latter may attract more viewers, but the slower-
paced programs communicate more and generally better content.

Nearly all the major concerns that parents should have about the
effects of TV content on their children are addressed implicitly in this
simple distinction between visual razzle-dazzle and real communication. Most of the more violent shows are also faster-paced, partly
because violence is one visual mechanism for increasing a program's
pace. Also, the faster shows are more likely to appeal to children who
probably shouldn't watch as much television because of learning difficulties, problems with hyperactivity and the like. In my judgment,
this simple distinction works partly because it reflects widely different
attitudes toward children on the part of the programs' makers, who
might see kids as a mere market to be conquered or as a group of
special people who represent an impressionable resource for humankind.

4. How can I promote reading among children? The most effective way
to promote childhood reading is to establish a family life that values
reading. Certainly this means limiting TV and radio or audiotape
time, but it requires a positive response as well. Most youngsters are
unlikely to become avid readers unless they see their parents reading,
they are encouraged by parents to read, their close friends read, and
reading is made a fun family activity.

This should begin when children are able to focus aurally on the
voices of their parents, usually between twelve and eighteen months
of age. Begin reading to your children appropriately simple stories
and poetry (rhymes). Hold the child while you read; let him or her
hear the warm resonance of your voice and feel the comforting security of your body. Audiotapes are also very helpful, but not as a
substitute for parental involvement. Some parents like to audiotape

their own readings for use when sitters are present. At about two years of age, large picture books become great fun because parents and children can interact about the book (for example, the parent can ask the child questions about the story and the little one can answer by pointing to details in the pictures).

By the time a child enters preschool, it's important to coordinate outside reading with family reading. Find out what books are being used at school, and read and discuss some of the same ones at home. Too often we treat school as a separate world, thereby losing both parental monitoring of school-media content and the opportunity to encourage a child's classroom work by integrating it into home life.

Finally, load up with reading material for periods when the electronic media are absent or inappropriate. These include car trips, family vacations and summertime, as well as daily periods when a child's boredom seems to be too much for him or her to handle. Today some excellent reading materials are available on computer as well, but unless you can swap programs with friends, rent them from libraries or borrow them from schools, you'll likely find the cost prohibitive. Libraries are great for books, if you can keep your youngest ones from chewing up or otherwise disfiguring the books. We also relied heavily on garage or yard sales, where we picked up hundreds of decent-quality hardcovers and paperbacks.

In spite of what you may have heard, reading is not a dead activity in North American culture. Quite the contrary: many younger parents are deeply interested in promoting literacy and the joy of reading among their children. One result is the growth of book "superstores" with much better children's literature sections than we had in bookshops when I was growing up. According to the American Booksellers Association, the book industry was the fastest-growing retail segment during the 1980s, behind only fast food. It would be more accurate to say that we are becoming a nation of readers and nonreaders rather than a land of just nonreaders. Parents are probably more responsible for this division than are teachers and the book industry.

Losing Balance

If parents make any major media blunders with their younger children, it is usually in maintaining a poor balance between low- and high-tech media. They use television and other media as baby sitters without considering the consequences for normal child development. Although the mass and new personal electronic media have a role even in childhood, the *relationships* between parents and children are crucial in the lives of young image-bearers of God. It is not enough that parents and children merely "get along." Parental love requires deep communication based on empathy, practiced through listening and enjoyed through daily interaction.

In many homes today the "listeners" are not parents but media celebrities, Big Bird, Barney and Mr. Rogers. Too many children feel as if their real friends are high-tech images. In their childish way they may feel that the media figure accepts them and is available every day for playful activities. By contrast, parents are either not immediately available or too preoccupied with other matters to give the child personal attention. High-tech personas don't require anything of the child. Nor do they speak scoldingly to him or her. They are accepting of every child who tunes in to their program or listens to their tape. These characters truly seem like friends.

When the child is emotionally needy, however, the significance of the parent is very clear. A crying little one cannot run to the high-tech personas, but looks instead to the comfort of an adult-in-the-flesh with outstretched arms and a warm, reassuring voice. Suddenly the balance shifts in favor of the actual parent—until the crisis is over.

In today's mass media world, the ease of preoccupying children with media is leading to a kind of "crisis parenting" that greatly devalues the parent-child relationship. Parents feel as if they are loving their young child merely by filling her or his time with technology and then making themselves available for sporadic crises. The parent is not so much a real nurturer as a manager of leisure technology, on the one hand, and of crisis, on the other.

My wife spent years visiting patients in their homes. Many of them were young parents whose little tykes ran through the house while she delivered various kinds of medical care. As she drove from one house to another, my wife concluded that relational parenting hardly exists among many of today's fathers and mothers. Especially in lower-income neighborhoods, the media blast away all day long, diverting attention away from parent-child relationships and toward the outside world as represented in movies, television and radio. Only a crisis— a smashed finger or a fight among siblings—may bring the parent back into the child's world.

A number of writers have referred to television as "the opiate of the masses." That metaphor captures the tube's ability to induce laziness and to divert human attention from the real world. But it misses the mark by overlooking the possible role of *all* mass media in making human beings nonrelational. Whether it's a book or a VCR, the latest issue of the *National Enquirer* or the latest episode of *Current Affair,* the fundamental question is essentially the same: How do we balance mass and interpersonal media for the good of the family?

Parental responsibilities outside the home vary from family to family, but it is hard to imagine a situation in which the children themselves would benefit from *more* mass communication and *less* interpersonal communication. As a general rule, then, regardless of how much leisure time parents actually have, we can ask whether the available time is used sufficiently to meet the emotional needs of the children. Parents who work full-time outside the home have an ominous obligation to try to get in as much "quality time" as possible with their families.

Creative Play

I have vivid memories of sprawling with my father on the living-room carpet, playing various games and "wrasslin'." I was probably four or five. Even though he was enormously busy trying to make a living, he felt a desire to give some of his time to me. To this day, I'm grateful for those moments of play, because my father's health was already deteriorating. There would not be many more times of creative play for the two of us.

So-called creative play is a dying art in many media-saturated families. Whether it's verbal or physical or both, creative play is two or more people interacting imaginatively for fun and fellowship. Creative play is the opposite of "consuming" media; it's "producing" your own experiences.

When my wife was growing up in suburban Chicago, she and a neighbor girl invented all kinds of games for themselves and area families. They collected backyard junk for their own miniature golf tournaments. They wrote and staged dramatic productions, puppet shows and musicals. They rounded up stuffed animals for their own zoos. In short, they imaginatively used the materials at hand to create enjoyable and relationship-building activities.

Today's children are much more likely to want other people to entertain them. From the earliest ages they are taught implicitly not to get in the way, not to make a mess and not to bother their parents. Childhood creativity has become more of a parental problem than a family resource. Frequently only goal-directed creativity, such as playing a musical instrument, is rewarded. Mere creative play seems to have no value.

Our parental priorities are greatly in need of repair. Creative play is not a bother, but essential for both the emotional and the overall cognitive development of children. Rather than discouraging it, we should help our offspring to begin exploring their God-given gifts through creative play with friends and family. Here are three rules for promoting play.

1. Show an interest. Children are much more likely to engage in creative play with each other and with parents if they feel that you are interested. Too many parents want their kids to play creatively but aren't willing to watch, listen or participate with the children. Youngsters like the play itself, but they especially enjoy the attention they receive from adults.

In my view, childlike creative play is a human reflex dating to God's command to take care of and develop the creation. Even though play is not income-producing work, it is human effort exerted upon the creation. Moreover, creative play has the winsome quality of life before the tragedy of the Fall, when work lost its joy and became drudgery and pain. No doubt some kinds of play can be mean and nasty, but much childhood creative play embodies a wonderful innocence. Certainly we should encourage this by giving it our attention and blessing.

2. Help stimulate ideas. Many times children generate their own ideas for creative play, but other times they need a little outside stimulation. How many times in the summer have you heard the kids chant, "I'm bored!" or "We don't know what to do"? These refrains are typical of children in a consumer culture, where so much leisure activity is programmed by the media rather than created by the kids.

As much as possible, we should help generate ideas for the kids' creative activities. My wife and I discovered a number of years ago that one of the most effective ways of doing this is simply telling the kids about our childhood play. Not only do they love to hear these stories, but the tales inspire them to generate their own modern-day versions. We believe that parents' personal recollections both serve as examples of play and, perhaps most important, implicitly tell children that such play is a good and worthwhile activity. Perhaps this is why our children most liked stories about play that seemed to challenge acceptable behavior, such as when my wife and her friends took wood from a neighbor's garage, along with an old tire, a fallen gutter and other trash, and turned it all into a backyard miniature golf course—and then charged a whopping two cents for neighborhood kids and adults to play.

Another way to help stimulate creative play is to suggest the availability of particular materials. It's amazing how simple props, such as a card table and blanket, can suddenly turn a lazy afternoon into an adventure in a new "fort." Rather than telling the children what to do, suggest the materials and let them come up with the games.

Although media-related materials can engender very creative play, in most instances such play is highly formulaic and imitative. Children will use TV-related character toys, for instance, to reenact what they've seen and heard on the tube. Their imaginations are directed by previous media experience. Truly creative play breaks this cycle of media dependence, opening the imagination to meaningful activities that come from the child's own experiences. In other words, creative play has the advantage of helping kids to work out their feelings and emotions by communicating them to others and to themselves in the very act of play.

When my wife was in a car accident a number of years ago, our children, then four and six, used play to reenact the accident and affirm their mother's safety. Repeatedly they put Barbie at the wheel of her plastic convertible and pushed her down the stairs, proudly pronouncing her "fine" after a postaccident inspection. We were able to use the play incidents to spark conversation with the children abou the real accident and their fears that they could have lost their mother.

Mr. Rogers, in my judgment the champion of young children's TV programming, has used the "Land of Make-Believe" roughly in this manner. Although he obviously guides the play by creating the imaginary characters and stories, the play is so strongly thematic that it can't help but stimulate a child's thought *about* the topic, whether it be friendship or divorce or fear. This creates an opportunity for parents to discuss these topics with their children, even if they are not personally confronting the issue being addressed on the show. Compared with most other children's programming, *Mr. Rogers' Neighborhood* probably elicits more creative thoughts and ideas even if it doesn't provide specific activities for creative play.

3. Parents need to participate sometimes. No matter how uncomfortable or silly it might seem at the time, parental participation in children's creative play is a healthy activity that will likely lead offspring to value and enjoy their parents as friends, not just as parents. When parents join in the fun, the children are honored and appreciative that adults would think enough of their play to become kids once again themselves. Parent-child creative play says to the children, "It's OK to be a child," and "My imagination can be a good thing." Such assurances are valuable in a world where children are frequently ignored or criticized by overworked, impatient adults.

Much has been written in recent years about the "loss of childhood," especially how the media rob children of innocence and push them into adult problems and issues long before they are really ready for them. While there is much to this argument, especially in a TV family, it has focused almost exclusively on the needs of kids at the risk of missing a valuable lesson about *adult* needs and experiences. Adults need to be childlike too. They too are robbed of their childlike qualities by immersion in the media world.

I learned this lesson firsthand. My childhood was not lighthearted and joyful, but filled with much hardship and pain. Not only did we struggle financially, but—more significantly—we tried to maintain a family amid the ravages of tuberculosis, alcoholism, a self-destructive marriage and other difficulties. As the youngest child, I encountered the effects of these problems as they got progressively worse. I was not completely robbed of a childhood, largely because I had some wonderful friends, but family problems were always in the back of my mind. Rarely did I play with pure joy and abandon.

Years later, with a marvelous marriage and two terrific children, I suddenly discovered that I could regain some of the childhood innocence I had lost three decades earlier. By the inexplicable grace of God, I was increasingly able to experience a joyous childhood vicariously through the lives of my kids. I could laugh and frolic with them, sharing in their innocent play and even feeling free to contribute creatively to their antics. At first it was not easy; I felt uncomfortable and awkward. But as the kids accepted this adult interloper in their midst, I began to let go—eliciting their delighted, gracious laughter.

Creative play is an opportunity for adults to reenter childhood, not just a chance for children to be themselves. I suspect that many readers of this book have felt the urge to play, but have not been able to abandon adult inhibitions. For the sake of the entire family, try letting go. Get down on the carpet, on a bike, in the grass or under the table. A day will come when the children will be driving cars and heading for college. Then you'll wish you had become a child once again. And so will the kids.

If all else fails, or if time has passed you by, watch for the grandkids. They'll get a real kick out of a childlike grandparent. And so will their parents!

The Peer Problem

Not long ago, after speaking at a large church, I was confronted with a problem that was relatively unheard-of in my childhood days but is increasingly common today: how to cope with the *indirect* influence of the media through peer groups. A young couple described how their three-year-old son had become a Batman fanatic even though he had never seen any of the Batman movies, TV shows or comics. His introduction to this make-believe character had come entirely from interaction with other kids, principally through play. Normally we think of peer influences among adolescents and especially teens, not among preschoolers. But the "peer problem" has taken on a much bigger dimension in the media world.

As the media moguls learn how to market their products to young children, we should expect more and more of this kind of situation. The characters and stories are popularized through toys, and children increasingly incorporate them into their imaginative play lives. As children then get together to play, the media products' values and beliefs are *indirectly* passed along from one peer group to another, from media-oriented children to less media-saturated kids. Before we know it, our children are full-fledged fans of media heroes we don't admire in the least.

The bad news is that it is impossible to control this process without limiting our kids' social relationships. We can't tell other parents what media are acceptable for their children, though we can discuss it with them tactfully and with plenty of space for disagreement. Nor can we totally select our children's friends, just as we can't choose our own neighbors, colleagues or fellow church members. It's amazing what kids can learn even from one hour weekly in the church nursery or during recess at school. Needless to say, preschool settings are very difficult to monitor, and it's much harder to evaluate the *kids* in a preschool than it is to evaluate the teachers and curriculum. All of these realities make it pretty tough to control peer influences.

The good news is that when children lack direct media experience, parents can more easily shape the ways they integrate the media world into their own experience. If our children haven't seen or heard the character for themselves, they are not deeply committed to any particular version of their media hero. I recommended to the family with the Batman-crazed son that they not make a big issue of the superhero. If they did, they would likely increase their son's interest in or fascination with Batman. Instead, I suggested that the father, who plays "hero" games with the child, simply divert the Batman character into his tales. By "playing Batman" matter-of-factly with his son, the father can define who the character is, what he stands for and what he does. In fact, this approach gives the family a chance not only to direct media-character play in a more acceptable way but possibly even to influence other children through the son's peer group.

The Video Craze

During the late 1980s electronic games took North American children by storm. Parents were caught off guard by the explosion of Nintendo and Sega games, probably because none of the earlier video games had achieved anything near such popularity. But the fact that parents gave in to the craze was unmistakable, since they bought the units in record numbers as Christmas gifts, birthday presents and "stop-the-whining" attempts to keep up with the Joneses' kids. By 1990 video games were being stocked widely by video-rental shops and even some libraries. According to practically all expert opinions, the video craze was not a onetime fad but an overnight movement of video gaming into mainstream family life. The craze began the ongoing spread of high-tech video and computer games into modern society.

There is little doubt, however, that one of the key factors in the willing intrusion of these technologies into family life was the complicity of fathers. As the hit TV show *Home Improvement* suggests, husband-fathers tend to be optimistic "gadgeteers" who display their manhood partly through the power afforded by tools and technology. Make no mistake about it, the video-game revolution is predominantly a male enterprise. While women of all ages focus more on relational activities, boys and men often gravitate toward largely nonrelational power games. For this reason we have to look at the video craze in the context of family life, not just in terms of childhood activities or kids' play.

Here again, there's a moderately good side to the story. In some homes, video games do bring fathers and sons together at least for media-oriented play. This might not seem to represent much benefit, but the fact is that in many families, almost anything that increases father-son interaction is an improvement. Also, even media-related play can lead to other shared activities and conversation about personal matters. Anytime a technology brings people together, there is the possibility of communication.

On the downside, though, too many video games are based on time-bound strategies that focus nearly all attention on the game and provide very little opportunity for discussion among participants. If the game controls time, it probably destroys more interpersonal communication than it fosters. The vast majority of popular video and com-

puter games are of this type, requiring players to act quickly within
set time limits. Incidentally, this is especially true of the kinds of video
games found in arcades and other public places.

Yet I remain optimistic that parents, including fathers, will see
what's happening with these technologies and will lend greater support to the companies trying to make new games that enhance parent-
child interaction and even provide educational value. Lewis Perelman, author of *School's Out: Hyperlearning, the New Technology and the
End of Education,* estimates that today about 99 percent of kids' real
learning takes place outside of the classroom. He includes the learning of such things as problem solving, social skills and language ac-
quisition. And he too is hopeful that the electronic superhighway will
benefit the child and the family and not just burn up valuable leisure
time with unproductive, noncreative play.

Those of us who attended school years ago and grew up in a largely
low-tech world find it hard to believe that the high-tech gadgets that
we associate with "mere" entertainment can also be used to teach and
train people. But video is not inherently a leisure-time pursuit or
amusement activity. Even critics such as Neil Postman, author of the
popular *Amusing Ourselves to Death,* underestimate the extent to which
the way we use a communications technology shapes its value in our
lives and determines its effects on our lives. As computer and video
technologies merge, there will be many opportunities for families to
use the new systems for distinctly educational and relational purposes.

Perhaps the best-known case of this so far is the remarkable popularity of the computer game "Where in the World is Carmen San
Diego?" By current standards it is not a very technologically sophisticated game, but its simple charm, relational uses and educational
goals have made it one of the most popular "educational" programs
ever marketed. Instead of relying on a time-bound strategy, the game

is paced slowly to provide for both user discussion and learning. Players track various unknown criminals around the world, using clues to determine where the criminals are located so the police can move in for the arrest. Players learn geography, industries, national flags and, in some versions, national anthems as well.

If we are willing to use them wisely, the new technologies can be a worthwhile contribution to family life. They can help parents create a home environment that makes learning fun, and we all know how difficult it is to communicate that message to children, who often associate formal education with boredom. They can help prepare children for using these technologies later in life, encouraging them to learn computer keyboarding and programming. They can bring the family together, including fathers and children. And in the best of circumstances, the video craze might force a family to come together to make hard choices about balancing high- and low-tech communication in a media world.

At Oyster River Elementary School in Durham, New Hampshire, creative teachers have come up with a wonderful means of both balancing and bridging high- and low-tech media. Fourth- and fifth-grade students make their own video documentaries about people and organizations in the area. In effect, they do primary research, learning interviewing skills and critical thinking as well as production techniques. They are not mere consumers of the tube but remarkably thoughtful producers of information and stories.

For the Children

Young children are a precious resource that requires care and nurture. This includes parental oversight of how and why they use various media. It takes time and energy for parents to do more than occasionally check out what their kids are watching, listening to and reading.

But the effort will pay dividends in families that balance the uses of media, and where parents try to understand each child's particular emotional needs.

I was both shocked and amused by my son's adventure with the heroic underpants. As I watched and listened to him, however, I increasingly understood his predicament as a growing boy in search of meaningful role models and moral direction. The episode taught me that mass media are not frivolous in a child's life, but are significant sources of values and beliefs. We had best keep this in mind as the electronic superhighways bring our youngsters into an ever-widening media world.

7

Wonder Years

Raising Teens in an Electronic Supermarket

Ⅰn the late 1950s my next-oldest brother bought a new car, and with it a new image. It was a 1955 Dodge sedan with a powerful V8 engine and an automatic transmission that didn't work in reverse. He promptly painted his chariot royal blue and slapped on moon hubcaps. It was an impressive vehicle, the envy of many high-school classmates.

Generally speaking, the car was off-limits to me, because it wasn't cool for my brother to get caught taking a spin with a kid brother in the car. But every once in a while a wave of inexplicable charity descended upon my sibling, who offered to take me along to the local teen hangout. In Des Plaines, Illinois, there was only one hangout, because the town was known for only one thing—it was the home of the first McDonald's restaurant franchise, located appropriately at

Five Corners, the most cosmopolitan spot in our suburban burg.

I'd sit in the back seat, the only acceptable place for a younger sibling, while my brother drove the land yacht north to the golden arches. Three or four blocks before we spotted the teenage mecca, I could always smell the first waves of grease, which activated my salivary glands as if I were one of Pavlov's dogs. My brother ritualistically made one loop through the parking lot before settling on a place to rest his cruiser. Where you parked said a lot about who you were.

What happened next remained a mystery to me for a few years. My brother left the car and proceeded to drift from one group of teens to another, frequently laughing but other times apparently discussing important matters. There were mostly guys, with a few girls who were "attached" to some of the bigger and more attractive males. Since there was no indoor seating in this early McDonald's, all of this action took place in the asphalt lot around and inside of various cars.

After an hour or more of this mysterious ritual, my brother would return to his own vehicle for the trip home. Several friends would push the car back into the center of the lot, and we'd roar onto the street, leaving behind plenty of smoking rubber. As near as I could figure, the smoke signal was a way of saying, "See ya later!"

Once we were out of sight of the arches, my brother looked in the mirror at me and said, "Hey, kid. Wanna few french fries?" He didn't need to ask, since I had been salivating during the entire time in the parking lot. But I still nodded in the mirror to my grinning sibling with the DA haircut. He always responded by slowly flicking one cold, stale fry after another over his shoulder and onto the seat or floor around me. Like the sparrows back in the drive-in parking lot, I dove after each one.

While I grabbed fries, my brother cranked up the car radio, which reverberated with top-40 hits on WLS. Elvis, the Four Seasons, the

Everly Brothers—they were broadcast over and over again in autos "tooling" up and down the strip to Five Corners. I recall only two major product commercials, for pizza and for acne medicine, interrupting the chatter of the DJ, Dick Biondi, and his radio jukebox of popular hits. Years later it finally dawned on me that the two products were symbiotic: greasy pizza helped spawn an enormous market for skin cleansers.

Two Adolescent Crises

I didn't know it back then, but I was about to lose my childhood innocence along with everybody else my age. By the time we entered high school, we knew we weren't kids anymore. It was somewhat embarrassing to ride a bike, so everybody hoped for an older friend with "wheels." But we certainly weren't adults. Few of us had real jobs or other adult responsibilities. Trapped between kidhood and adulthood, we were part of the generationally segmented group known as adolescents.

Adolescence can be an awful lot of fun, but as any adult remembers, it is also one of the most awkward and frustrating times of life. Hormones create new feelings and strange desires, especially toward the opposite sex. Friendships are important but often hard to develop and maintain. Parents are a "pain"; they don't seem to know when to give freedom and when to provide structure and rules. Parental discipline is both appreciated and disliked.

In these tumultuous times, when the rules of life seem so much up for grabs, two crises stalk adolescents day and night. The first and most fundamental is the crisis in *identity*. A "normal" adolescent is more or less uncomfortable with himself or herself—with looks, behavior, voice—and yearns to be someone different, someone "better" in the eyes of peers. Teenagers are seekers of a sense of self, looking for a manageable and likable image of themselves in a sea of uncertainty.

Adolescents are also seekers of *intimacy*. They want to have close emotional relationships, often with people of the opposite sex. Girls apparently feel this need more than do adolescent males, but it is a significant crisis for both genders. The problem, of course, is that childlike expressions of intimacy, such as sitting on a parent's lap or hugging a close friend in public, are embarrassing to American teens, who want their space. On the other hand, fully adult expressions of intimacy are awkward and often even frightening. To make matters even more difficult, physical and emotional intimacy are often wrongly linked only to sexuality.

These two crises, the drive for intimacy and the search for identity, are hallmarks of the postchildhood, preadulthood years. As the age of puberty falls in Western society, and as these crises extend into later years, adolescence becomes a longer and longer period of life.

From a male perspective, female adolescence seems like an ageless virus caught by more and more women. Every time I go to the local shopping mall I feel greater confusion: older women seem to be acting and dressing like younger and younger ones, while ever younger girls seem to be dressing and acting like older ones. Their crises become mine, as I'm not always sure when childhood ends and adulthood begins. I didn't know whether to smile or frown when President Clinton's daughter, Chelsea, decided for her thirteenth birthday that she wanted to see the PG-13 rated film *Untamed Hearts*.

The Media Solution

In this type of adolescent culture, where identities are up for grabs and where adult-adolescent communication is weak, the media play an unprecedented role in teenage life. First, the media challenge the authority of parents, pastors and teachers. Teens look to media celebrities for styles of dress, acceptable behavior, and even values and beliefs to guide their lives. Rock-music stars, television characters and radio personalities are mentors and teachers, not just entertainers. Sometimes one celebrity, such as a Madonna, truly becomes an idol who is imitated by millions of youth. Viewing movies is an especially powerful way for adolescents to feel vicariously like an adult by experiencing the emotions of slightly older characters. The teen can sample adulthood, thereby pretending to be as much of an authority on life as are his or her parents.

Second, the media not only challenge traditional sources of authority but also redefine them. In other words, young people "learn" about parents, teachers, pastors and other adult role models by consuming mass media. Teen films, for instance, tend to instruct adolescents about dealing with inflexible parents, wimpy pastors and moronic schoolteachers. For every smart, caring adult in teen flicks, there are dozens of idiotic or controlling ones. The lesson is clear: adults are a problem, not an aid to growing up. Partly because of real adults' absence in teens' lives and partly because of negative media portrayals of adults, many youth participate very little in the adult world.

Interestingly, the common media depiction of severe alienation between parents and children is simply not reality. Instead, numerous studies have found there is a lack of communication because adults are often not available and because youth don't seek out adults. Parents are too busy pursuing their own goals in work and leisure, while adolescents are busily consuming media and communicating with their peer groups.

The media, then, serve as quasi-educational "adults" in teens' lives. Adolescents look to the media implicitly for advice about how to achieve a likable identity and to gain intimate relationships. And frequently youth do this together by going to the same movies, listening to the same radio stations and recorded music, reading the same magazines and novels, and watching the same television programs.

I can recall vividly from my own middle-school days how inadequate I felt compared with the contemporary male icons who appealed to girls in my classes. Girls used to carry around photos of their current idols—rock stars and television heroes such as Lee Majors—in their school notebooks. In those days I couldn't figure out why girls were more interested in guys they would never meet than they were in male classmates who would have loved a little feminine attention. It would have made sense to me, however, if I had considered the concurrent male dilemma: our male heroes were some of the same figures from the media world. We chased for ourselves the same media-fabricated identities that girls idolized.

The Sex Connection

The media-saturated teen culture is understandably obsessed with sexuality. Unfortunately, we parents spend too much time lamenting the sexual content of adolescent media and far too little time trying to understand it. Since the crises of identity and intimacy occur during puberty, the physical and emotional aspects of adolescent culture are nearly always tangled in the same media webs.

I'll never forget the time a middle-aged father told me he simply could not understand why his teenage daughter watched soap operas. He was not only concerned but thoroughly befuddled. Because *he* had no desire to watch soaps, he assumed that something must be wrong with his daughter. His attitude reflected a lack of empathy as well as healthy concern. I wondered whether he had ever spoken with his daughter about sexuality, not just about soaps. When I asked him this question, he turned red and babbled an unintelligible answer.

For many youth, the media are an educational window that overlooks the adult world. Adolescents can peer curiously through that window to get a private peek at adult identity and adult intimacy. Parents might not talk with them about these matters, but the media will gladly provide a few private lessons. Research shows, for instance, that North American teens turn to the media and to peers for sex education before they turn to parents, pastors, teachers and other adults—often even before they will turn to a sibling.

The creators of teen-oriented media know how significant sexuality is to adolescents. They realize that sex draws teen audiences, not because most teens are sex-crazed or because adolescents care only about sexuality but because sex is one of the most emotionally compelling ways of addressing teenage desires for identity and intimacy. As my colleagues and I showed in *Dancing in the Dark*, the success of the first rock-music channel, MTV, was due significantly to the way its creators established a sense of personal relationship between on-air "VJs" and lonely teen viewers. Female VJs appealed to male as well as female viewers, while male rock stars on the channel's videos were "invited" personally into viewers' bedrooms and family rooms. Even the early MTV sets were created to resemble apartments, bedrooms or lofts. In its most intimate programming, MTV turns viewers into voyeurs of rich and famous teen idols.

The same sexually oriented appeals are used across the spectrum of adolescent media. Television's *Beverly Hills 90210*, among the most popular teen programming ever on the tube, addressed sexuality in episode after episode. Girls' magazines often use advice columns and fiction to address sexual themes. Rock-station DJs increasingly use sexually oriented humor, while the stations' news staffs hunt for sexually oriented reports—to say nothing of the lyrics of popular music. Teen flicks, long the staple of dates and adolescent drama, probably address intimate relationships more than any other theme. Bradley Greenburg of Michigan State University estimates that American teens are exposed to up to four thousand sexual references every year on television and in movies. He discovered that R-rated movies have an average of seventeen sex scenes, with half of them featuring intercourse between unmarried partners. Even teen romance novels have become steamier in recent decades.

Fallen Gender Ideals

Today's teens grow up under enormous pressure to conform to particular cultural ideals that are portrayed over and over again in the media. Fashion, language and hair styles change quickly, but overarching views of maleness and femaleness are moving clearly in opposite directions. Male identity is patterned after power, what I call the "butt-kicking he-man." Female identity is tied to a proper figure, perfect complexion and other physical "attractiveness," what I call the "plastic female." Both of these cultural ideals link identity and intimacy to external expressions of sexuality, thereby challenging the biblical view of persons as image-bearers of God.

Adolescent males are pounded by the media to see their value in terms of how much power they have over other people, males and females alike. There are very few media expressions of men as sensitive, compassionate servants who are *granted* authority by others. Rather, the media male, especially in teenage media, is usually the person who *takes* authority by lording it over others. He's the football hero on Sunday afternoons, the beer guzzler on commercial breaks, the automobile driver spinning around mountain curves in a sports car. He's the young corporate star climbing the company's ladder or the high-school celebrity who outfoxes the teachers and principal. He gets the girl, by hook or by crook, and drives into the sunset in his chariot of steel. His symbols of power are automobiles, electronics—let's not forget the amplified guitar—and the fist, which can throw a ball, fire a gun or level an opponent.

I've long studied beer commercials, which in my judgment are among the most telling cultural icons of manhood. Many people believe that teens drink alcoholic beverages because of peer pressure, to escape from poor home situations or simply to have a good time. No doubt these are all factors. But I believe the majority of beer commercials tell (and teach) another story: alcohol is among the most powerful means for males to express their "macho" instincts in a fallen world. Alcohol creates in males an enhanced sense of power and authority, even while it deadens the senses. Beer in particular has become the nectar of manhood, with males sharing their misdirected authority by imbibing together in the "fellowship" depicted on commercials. Teen pics are sprinkled liberally with drunkenness, and some rock groups—usually the more macho ones—booze it up for fun and image. It shouldn't surprise us that beer consumption has become one of the major rites of passage for many male adolescents.

If males are after power, females follow their own, equally wicked adolescent appointments with a gender-oriented idol. Over and over again, to the point of satiety, the media focus on women's bodies. We see this ideal "bod" on billboards, on the tube and in the movies. The same ideal appears repeatedly in women's magazines, in both editorial and advertising content. It's impossible to miss the point: women are what they look like, not what they can accomplish or what they value and believe. Their looks are their essence, for their body determines their identity as well as their image in the minds of family members and especially peers. Without the proper look, identity and intimacy will never be satisfactorily achieved. Susan Harter of the University of Denver found that even for children the most important factor in self-esteem is physical appearance, especially for girls. Seymour Fisher, a New York psychiatrist, says, "Even by the age of 5, girls rate their bodies' attractiveness less favorably than boys do."

The pressure on young women to meet this ideal is enormous. If their skin is not "pure," their figure is out of proportion or their hair is "unmanageable," they can suffer low self-esteem. The mysterious ideal, which seems to achieve "reality" only in the media, sets the unattainable standard by which women unfavorably compare themselves. Young women try to beat their bodies into submission with cycles of dieting, shopping for image-altering clothing, rounds of cosmetics and endless glamour advice from magazines and talk shows.

When positive measures don't work, younger and younger females turn to self-destructive behaviors. They have high rates of smoking, substance abuse, sexually transmitted diseases and especially eating disorders. More than 90 percent of eating disorders occurs among females. Over half of adolescents believe they are fat, and one out of five adolescent women in North America reports using diet pills to lose weight. Some young women even become pregnant partly to give meaning to their lonely lives. Yet all these activities lead adolescent women even further from the media ideal.

Each of these cultural ideals is problem enough for adolescent males and females. Taken together, however, they are mutually destructive. The young guy learns that "real men" lord it over women, and he counts his intimate conquests on the way to a manly identity. The young woman, in turn, preens herself for the "victory" of the conquest that will make her life worse. She is the plastic woman, putting on any façade that will sell the male on her body. A Camp Fire Youth Survey in 1992 found that only 69 percent of adolescents believe that a girl has the right to refuse sex, even at the last minute. Thirty-one percent aren't sure it's rape if a girl agrees to have sex but says no at the last minute and is forced to continue. When the cultural ideals establish the parameters for adolescent sexuality, these data are entirely understandable.

Instead of getting better, or even staying the same, the cultural idols are pushing adolescents further into impossible and self-destructive roles. Researchers at American University found, for instance, that body measurements of women in *Playboy* magazine and Miss America contests, along with the female images in diet and exercise magazines, have generally decreased. Body weight for these women was 13 to 19 percent below the weight expected for women of their ages. According to the American Psychiatric Association, weight of more than 15 percent below normal is one symptom of anorexia nervosa. In other words, by trying to please men as well as themselves, women have followed a cultural ideal that makes it more difficult for them to control their own lives.

If all of this were not bad enough, the plastic female is also increasingly depicted as an immodest, sexually suggestive girl. Younger and younger women are dressed more or less like Madonna, the whorish babe in clothing that resembles lingerie. MTV and teen flicks are fashion-conscious channels of sexual desire.

The overall trend in our media-saturated society is for adolescents to become more and more outwardly driven toward these fallen idols. Instead of finding self-esteem from who they are on the inside as created by God, they furiously work to become a somebody in the eyes of others, creating a "mediagenic" image as a butt-kicking male or a plastic female. Without any personal anchors in family traditions, religious absolutes and community or congregational life, they are highly susceptible to their own delusions about happiness—delusions formed largely by the media and peer groups. Where other voices are weak or nonexistent, media voices speak with power and conviction.

In the Christian family, adolescents need to hear over and over again the simple truth of the Scriptures that God looks at "the heart," not at the exterior image (1 Samuel 16:7). As Debra Evans suggests in *Beauty and the Best,* the Bible does not pay homage to physical beauty, let alone to media-promoted physical icons of maleness and femaleness. This truth has the power to liberate adolescents from the impossible, shifting standards generated in the media world—but only if adults communicate this truth patiently and honestly.

Consuming Images

Behind these destructive images of adolescent identity and intimacy is the canon of a consumer culture: "We are what we can buy." This is becoming the great credo of North American youth. From the time they first realize that money can at least temporarily buy happiness and pleasure, they begin linking consumption with the good life and ultimately with self-worth. Money becomes the tool for creating one's mediagenic identity and the resulting intimacy. Even the shoes one wears are a statement of who one is.

In this consumerism, shopping malls are appropriate places for adolescents to hang out. Many adolescents work, but not primarily to save money as much as to be able to spend it. *Newsweek* rightly called adolescent work and buying a "frenzy of consumerism." Teens earned about ninety-five *billion* dollars in 1991, according to Teenage Research Unlimited. They spent eighty-two billion! Few parents can afford to consume at that rate. In fact, many teens are better dressed than their parents. And where there's not cash, there is increasingly teenage credit. According to MasterCard International, about 10 percent of high-school juniors and seniors have regular access to a credit card in their name or their parents' name. The credit companies now realize that lifelong consumption patterns are set before college, and they are pushing competitively to get their products into the eager hands of high-school students.

For all of the benefits of teenage employment, the temptation to turn such work into a means of creating a consumerist identity should raise sobering questions with parents. Do our adolescents want to work in order to gain experience, learn responsibility and increase maturity? Or do they see work primarily as a way to get the cash that will help them to build a mediagenic identity? I see and hear about the latter more and more these days. Unfortunately, many parents easily capitulate, partly because they believe that work will still produce positive benefits even if the teens' goal is merely to make money, and partly because teenage income lessens the pressure on parents to buy the same products for their youth. Work *seems* like a winner on both counts, but in a consumer culture we should not be nearly so optimistic.

Perhaps volunteerism is a far better way of achieving the elusive goals of work. I've seen over and over again that teenagers who voluntarily serve others are much less likely to be caught up in the media world and consumerism. Their identities are generally more stable, and their values are much more selfless. With this in mind, doesn't it make sense for churches to lead the way by providing inspiring opportunities for youth to serve others rather than consume for themselves?

A few years ago I suggested to one rather affluent church that the leaders consider abandoning plans for the youth group to go to an amusement park for a few days during spring break. Instead, I suggested, the church could take the same funds and equip the youth and their adult mentors to donate time to a service project, such as repairing inner-city homes or assisting victims of a natural disaster. I've seen how this kind of experience can turn a teen's ephemeral consumerism into productive ministry—with life-changing results.

Work Versus Leisure

Adolescents learn early in their lives that work is unpleasant and that leisure is the best part of life. Household chores are a "drag," for instance, while movies and shopping are fun. By fifth or sixth grade, most youth have learned from the surrounding youth culture that school is fun only as a place to meet friends and socialize, not as a place to do schoolwork. Their lifelong approach to work and leisure is being formed: do minimum work for maximum leisure time. Years later, the same philosophy will influence their adult attitude: work is an unpleasant necessity that generates the money for much-sought leisure activities.

Adolescents' leisure-oriented philosophy wouldn't be very significant except for its impact on self-esteem and, ultimately, identity. Young people need to know that they have gifts and talents that can make a difference in the world. Leisure activities give them something to do, and the physical exertion might even be healthy, while the recreation is often therapeutic. Compared with some types of work, however, leisure rarely creates a sense of accomplishment. This is because leisure is usually based on consumption, while work is based on production. A teen who rarely produces anything cannot help but feel unfulfilled and in some cases even worthless.

The value of work is not limited to gainful employment. In fact, many of the typical teen jobs, such as those in fast-food restaurants, are tedious and uncreative. Youth may learn some responsibility in this sort of work, but it's not likely to make special use of their individual abilities, let alone help them feel that they have really helped other people. Other kinds of work, such as summer-camp counseling and baby-sitting, are potentially more beneficial.

Nevertheless, teen "work" is too narrowly defined in many families. Income is not the crucial factor, except of course where youth have to bring home a check to pay for their own clothes or other essentials. Rather, the use of a teen's abilities should be the most important consideration in decisions about worthwhile work. Volunteer work is a very valuable option, and it might include neighborhood or county clean-up programs, assisting at church programs, serving meals or distributing food items to the poor, and so on.

In recent years my wife and I were delighted to see this spirit of volunteerism in our children's Christian schools. The school staff introduced various service projects. Students could earn the necessary "credit" by participating in creek clean-ups or other volunteer projects. Meanwhile, the projects were discussed in appropriate classes, such as social studies or science. We were amazed at how enthusiastically our children participated and how much self-esteem they seemed to derive from such simple programs. If only we could convince them of the vital service to the community pro-vided by people who clean their rooms, cut the grass and wash the car!

According to experts on adolescence, too many parents virtually lock their children into a cycle of forced leisure. Although the kids are sometimes called upon to assist with special projects, the rest of the time it's boredom and leisure as usual. Parents are too lazy to help their offspring find worthwhile work, or they are simply oblivious to the role of work in adolescent self-esteem. They carry the baby-sitting-by-TV model into adolescence, substituting recordings and video-tapes, if not cars and cash. Even if the kids don't get into trouble in this kind of system, they are not helped to become productive members of society.

If nothing else is possible in your situation, try inviting your children to participate in mundane tasks by adding something relationally significant. For example, invite them along for grocery shopping, with the promise of some special time together afterward over a cup of coffee and a glass of soda at a nearby restaurant. If things go smoothly, you might "offer" to let the child cook a meal or plan the menu for an upcoming family dinner.

Our family has done just about everything together, from yard work to redecorating. Given some authority, such as the right to decide what kind of bush or tree to plant, our children have usually risen to the occasion by providing their fair share of work. This has made housework far more fun and relational, which helps us parents do our chores too.

When we moved a few years ago, we let our teenagers plan their own bedroom redecorating. We set the budget and suggested what had to be redecorated and what could remain the same (such as wood trim). We also provided the wheels to get them around to look at paints, carpets and paper. They then planned the projects, and we bought the materials. After some negotiation to guarantee no major problems (like mismatched carpet and paint), my wife and I did the work that they were not able to do competently and enlisted their talents on the rest. Their work made the rooms their own. And they were proud of those rooms.

Similarly, when my wife and I began working on the first edition of *The Best Family Videos*, we decided to include our adolescent children in the entire project. They were our reviewers of children's videos as well as our "consultants" on how to write the guide in a way that would be helpful to families with adolescents. Their advice was amazingly candid and helpful, and we eventually decided to dedicate the book to them. Not surprisingly, they were proud of the book when it rolled off the presses for the first time.

Schoolwork and the Media

The connection between school performance and adolescent media use has long been a concern among parents, educators and scholars—and rightly so. Since the media consume about one-third of a teenager's waking hours, far more than any other leisure activity, it stands to reason that the media must have an impact on study habits if not homework performance and grades. Indeed, one influential study of ninth-graders found a negative relationship between academic achievement and time spent listening to music and radio, while there was a positive relationship between overall academic performance and time spent on leisure reading. As MTV expands around the globe, as cable TV offers more adolescent programming, as teens get their own VCRs and portable stereos, the school performance of youth is likely to decline ever further.

A bit of chronology will help explain what's happening in this media-rich, school-poor environment. At about ten years of age, typical American preadolescents begin shifting from television to recorded music, radio, movies and videocassettes. Before long they spend four to six hours daily with music media and movies. When this happens, they begin leaving the media environment of the family and stepping out on their own with peers. They watch less and less TV with other family members, preferring to submerge themselves in a distinctly adolescent media world. In their minds, all of the "rewards" for media use are related to peers, not siblings or parents. They want to fit in with and impress their peers, as well as to sneak a few peeks at adult life through the media window.

Popular music and teen pics seem like valuable activities to adolescents. Music helps them express feelings to themselves and friends. Films give them stories that they can discuss with peers, especially stories about adolescent situations such as boy-girl relations and loneliness. In other words, these types of media help teens relate to each other but simultaneously lure them away from family and other adults, such as teachers and pastors.

One result is teens' disinterest in academics. Formal schooling, including reading, is associated with the adult world, whereas the electronic media are associated with the peer group and leisure. So youth often turn from academics as they pull away from parents and other adult authority figures. Some churches try to overcome this by hiring a young, energetic youth pastor who promises a relational ministry. And some of these pastors succeed in meeting the kids on their own turf by spending leisure time with them. Overall, however, youth ministers are simply not able to offset the lack of other adult role models. A few Bible studies and other church education programs, even if they interest youth, can't easily break the spell of adolescent media, let alone greatly increase the teenagers' desire to do well in school.

My point here is very important for parents who are concerned about their teenagers' school performance. The problem is *not* the media per se. Rather, the villain is a complex of factors, including generational segregation, an emphasis on leisure, parental disinterest, church irrelevance and peer relationships. For most kids, taking away their media technologies will not greatly improve their school performance (there is a better chance of this with early school-age kids). Instead it is important to bridge the generation gap, encourage parent-child colearning, establish relational teen ministries and cultivate learning as an enjoyable and rewarding activity. In this type of environment, the media are no longer so important and all-consuming.

Of all adults in a teenager's life, parents are in the best position to make this happen. They can give time for help with homework. They can provide opportunities for teens to work, and they can praise offspring for jobs well done or give additional assistance when needed. They can take enough interest in their church's youth ministry to determine how warmly relational or coldly academic it really is. By reading and discussing school-related materials with their children, they can show that they too value learning.

Over the years my wife and I have tried to make our family a learning environment by practicing these techniques. I admit that it's not always been easy. There have been *many* times when our first impulse was to entertain the kids with media products. As we have turned vacations and evenings into family learning experiences, however, we've kept alive our own desire to grow. I don't know how many times I've said to myself, for example, *I wish I could go back to school to study physics or chemistry.* Instead I read on my own, share what I learn with family and thereby make my peace with curiosity. Do you feel that way? Is learning fun? Do you wish you could go back to school? Your answers to these kinds of questions say a lot about how your own teens probably feel about school.

All the new technologies discussed in chapter four hold considerable potential for enhanced learning in the home as well as in school. I fear that in most homes this potential will be lost on leisure-time media or generationally defined entertainment. Parents are the key. If we don't guide and nurture our offspring on the new electronic superhighway, they will take the technology for a leisurely spin around the block or for an extended park in the garage—if not on lover's lane.

Empathy and Independence

In a survey of eight thousand students aged ten to twenty, the three most worrisome things they said they faced were school performance (56 percent), their looks (53 percent) and how well others liked them

(48 percent). These findings from *You and Your Adolescent* say a great deal about teens in a media world. Trying to manage all of their turbulent relationships, they're not sure that they can take care of academics too. Their identities are up for grabs, their looks are uncertain. And through it all they want others to like them, perhaps even intimately. These are heady concerns.

As I browsed through the parenting books on bookstore shelves, I was struck by the common denominator in the teen sections. Behind all the cute terms and gimmicky strategies for adolescent parenting was one major theme: *Patiently make yourself available for regular communication, especially listening.* So I'm delighted to report that some of the most recent studies of adolescence support this simple but timeless approach to teen parenting. It seems from recent research that both parents and scholars have overestimated the real rebelliousness of teens. Most adolescents don't want to push adults out of their lives, but they do want enough freedom to grow up and to become adults themselves. They want parents to be close with them, to share their problems with them and even—believe it or not—to be approachable for advice and counsel.

Adolescents want loving and interested parents with open arms, finely tuned ears and empathic hearts. But they are also worried that parents will smother them with adulthood and ruin their adolescence. That's all!

Our teens need us, and they know it. And we need them too. They are our next generation of leadership in churches and schools, business and government. Let's face it, youth are the principal national—and international—resource for the future of the human race and the kingdom of God. Shall we give them ourselves, or shall we turn to our own leisure and work vices while they flounder in a turbulent sea of ephemeral media identities? With all the uncertainty and pressures adolescents face in today's world, they should be able to count on us to tell them over and over again what God has already done for them: he made them *very good,* and he redeemed them at Calvary. Compared with these great truths, all of the media talk and images are hot air.

These were the truths I needed to hear back in Chicago during my own adolescent years. As the top-40 radio stations sprouted up across the land, fast-food restaurants began lining the main drags, drive-in theaters poked their screens out of former farm fields and transistor radios dotted the beaches, I too looked around for identity and intimacy. For a while I figured my brother must have found them. After all, he had wheels. But thousands of stale french fries later, I was not so sure that he or any other teens knew for certain.

But if my brother settled for a car that didn't work in reverse, I could settle for a lot less than the media said I needed. Who would have thought that Christ would give away more? The kingdom is around the corner from acne and pizza, if we would just serve it to our adolescents to the tune of love.

Bibliography

Selected Sources

"The American Family Time Satisfaction Study." Sponsored by Massachusetts Mutual Life Insurance Company and *Family Fun* magazine. November 1993.

"American Federation of Teachers/Chrysler Corporation Report on Kids, Parents and Reading." 1993.

Anderson, Richard C., et al. "Growth in Reading and How Children Spend Their Time Outside of School." *Reading Research Quarterly* 23 (Summer 1988): 283-305.

Arterburn, Stephen. *Toxic Faith: Understanding and Overcoming Religious Addiction.* Nashville: Oliver-Nelson, 1991.

Atkin, David J., et al. "The Home Ecology of Children's Television Viewing: Parental Mediation and the New Video Environment." *Journal of Communication* 41 (Summer 1991): 40-52.

Austin, Erica Weinstraub. "Exploring the Effects of Active Parental Mediation of Television Content." *Journal of Broadcasting & Electronic Media* 37 (Spring 1993): 147-58.

Beentjes, Johannes W. J., and Tom H. A. Van der Voort. "Television's Impact on Children's Reading Skills: A Review of Research." *Reading Research Quarterly* 23 (Fall 1991): 389-413.

Benware, Paul. "Closer and Deeper." *Moody,* September 1993, pp. 38-43.

Berg, Elizabeth. "Why I Hate Video Games." *Parents,* September 1992, p. 62.

Betcher, R. William, and William S. Pollack. *In a Time of Fallen Heroes: The Recreation of Masculinity.* New York: Atheneum, 1993.

Boorstin, Daniel J. *The Americans: The Democratic Experience.* New York: Vintage Books, 1974.

Briner, Bob. *Roaring Lambs: A Gentle Plan to Radically Change Your World.* Grand Rapids, Mich.: Zondervan, 1993.

"Buying a Computer for Your Kid Is Child's Play—Almost." *Business Week,* May 10, 1993, p. 89.

Carnegie Council on Adolescent Development, Task Force on Youth Development and Community Programs. "A Matter of Time: Risk and Opportunity in the Nonschool Hours." March 1993.

Coignard, Sophie. "Computers, TV and the Super-Child." *World Press Review,* March 1992, pp. 26-27.

Coles, Robert. *The Spiritual Life of Children.* Boston: Houghton Mifflin, 1990.

Colino, Stacey. "Turning Up the Volume." *American Health,* July/August 1993, p. 40.

Condry, John. "Thief of Time, Unfaithful Servant: Television and the American Child." *Daedalus* 122 (Winter 1993): 259-78.

Csikszentmihalyi, Mihaly, and Reed Larson. *Being Adolescent: Conflict and Growth in the Teenage Years.* New York: BasicBooks, 1984.

"Dobson's New Dare." *Christianity Today,* February 8, 1993, pp. 69-70.

Dombro, Amy. *The Ordinary Is Extraordinary: How Children Under Three Learn.* New York: Fireside, 1989.

Evans, Debra. *Beauty and the Best.* Colorado Springs, Colo.: Focus on the Family Publishers, 1993.

"Excess Idle Time Perils Youths, Study Shows." *Grand Rapids Press,* December 10, 1992, pp. A1, A4.

Fine, Gary Alan, et al. "Leisure, Work and the Mass Media." In *At the Threshold: The Developing Adolescent,* ed. S. Shirley Feldman and Glen R. Elliott. Cambridge, Mass.: Harvard University Press, 1990.

Gardner, James E. "Does Your Teen-ager Need a $95 Shirt—or Just Want One?" *TV Guide,* May 4, 1985, pp. 35-37.

Gettman, Katrina. "Quantity Time." *World,* January 8, 1994, p. 26.

Golin, Mark. "Are Video Games Zapping Your Child's Mind?" *Prevention,* August 1992, pp. 56-58.

Gortmaker, Steven L., et al. "The Impact of Television Viewing on Mental Aptitude and Achievement: A Longitudinal Study." *The Public Opinion Quarterly* 54 (Winter 1990): 594-604.

Greenberg, Bradley S., et al. *Media, Sex and the Adolescent.* Cresskill, N.J.: Hampton, 1993.

Griswold, Robert L. *Fatherhood in America: A History.* New York: BasicBooks, 1993.

Haglund, Rick. "Book Superstores Defy 'Nobody Reads' Myth." *Grand Rapids Press,* November 22, 1992, p. D5.

Hamburg, David A. "The Opportunities of Early Adolescence." *Teachers College Record* 94 (Spring 1993): 466-86.

Haves, Donald S., and Dina M. Casey. "Young Children and Television: The

Retention of Emotional Reactions." *Child Development* 63 (December 1992): 1428-36.

"Home, Home on the Remote: Does Fascination with TV Technology Create Male-Dominated Family Entertainment?" *Media & Values,* Fall 1992, pp. 21-24.

"How Americans Use Time: An Interview with Sociologist John P. Robinson." *The Futurist* 25 (September/October 1991): 23-27.

Howard, J. Grant. *The Trauma of Transparency: A Biblical Approach to Interpersonal Communication.* Portland, Ore.: Multnomah Press, 1979.

"Is It Rape?" *Dallas Morning News,* July 1, 1992, p. 5C.

Jablow, Martha M. *A Parent's Guide to Eating Disorders and Obesity.* New York: Delta, 1992.

Kantrowitz, Barbara. "An Interactive Life." *Newsweek,* May 31, 1993, pp. 42-44.

Kesler, Jay. "Giving Kids Tastes of Freedom." *Moody,* June 1992, pp. 53-54.

Kornheiser, Tony. "Control Freaks" [men's use of remote controls]. *Ladies' Home Journal,* April 1993, p. 108.

Krendl, Kathy A., et al. "Preschoolers and VCRs in the Home: A Multiple Methods Approach." *Journal of Broadcasting & Electronic Media* 37 (Summer 1993): 293-312.

Lacher, Irene. "MTV Generation Stumps Publishers." *Grand Rapids Press,* December 27, 1992, p. B7.

Landau, Steven, et al. "Visual Attention to and Comprehension of Television in Attention-Deficit Hyperactivity Disordered and Normal Boys." *Child Development* 63 (August 1992): 928-37.

Markoff, John. "The Keyboard Becomes a Hangout for a Computer-Savvy Generation." *The New York Times,* August 3, 1993, pp. A1, C5.

Mead, Margaret. *Culture and Commitment: A Study of the Generation Gap.* Garden City, N.Y.: American Museum of Natural History/Natural History Press, 1970.

Meier, Barry. "Credit Cards on the Rise in High Schools." *The New York Times,* September 5, 1992, p. 14.

Meyrowitz, Joshua. *No Sense of Place: The Impact of Electronic Media on Social Behavior.* New York: Oxford University Press, 1985.

Miller, Norma L. "Are Computers Dangerous to Children's Health?" *The Education Digest* 16 (June 1993): 62-65.

Mornell, Pierre. *Thank God, It's Monday: Or, How to Prevent Success from Ruining Your Marriage.* New York: Bantam, 1985.

Mutz, Diana C., et al. "Reconsidering the Displacement Hypothesis: Television's Influence on Children's Time Use," *Communication Research* 20 (February 1993): 51-75.

Myers, David G. *The Pursuit of Happiness: Who Is Happy—and Why.* New York: Morrow, 1992.

Nickel, Gordon. "The Joys of a TV-Free Summer." *Focus on the Family,* June 1994, pp. 6-7.

Norman, Jan. *The Private Life of the American Teenager: The Norman/Harris Report.* New York: Rawson, Wade, 1981.

"The Not-Ready-for-Prime-Time Prayers." *Harper's,* May 1993, p. 12.

Novak, Michael. "Television Shapes the Soul." In *Mass Media Issues,* ed. Leonard L. Sellers and William L. Rivers (Englewood Cliffs, N.J.: Prentice-Hall, 1977).

Overbeck, Joy. "Sex, Kids and the Slut Look." *Newsweek,* July 26, 1993, p. 8.

Perelman, Lewis J. *School's Out: Hyperlearning, the New Technology and the End of Education.* New York: Morrow, 1992.

Postman, Neil. *Amusing Ourselves to Death: Public Discourse in the Age of Show Business.* New York: Penguin, 1986.

Provenzo, Eugene P. "What Do Video Games Teach?" *The Education Digest* 58 (December 1992): 56-58.

"Putting Parents in the Loop with Kids and Computers: An Interview with Educational Software Designer Tom Snyder." *Home-Office Computing,* March 1989, pp. 80-83.

Relin, David Oliver. "Four Decades of Viewing Families." *Scholastic Update* (Teachers' Edition) 124 (September 6, 1991): 22.

Rifkin, Glenn. "Inventing Heroes for the 21st Century." *The New York Times,* February 14, 1993, p. 10.

Roberts, Donald F. "Adolescents and the Mass Media: From 'Leave It to Beaver' to 'Beverly Hills 90210.' " *Teachers College Record* 94 (Spring 1993): 629-44.

Robinson, John P. "As We Like It." *American Demographics* 15 (February 1993): 44-48.

———. "I Love My TV." *American Demographics* 12 (September 1990): 24-27.

———. "The Leisure Pie." *American Demographics* 12 (November 1990): 39.

———. "Thanks for Reading This." *American Demographics* 12 (May 1990): 6-7.

———. "The Time Squeeze." *American Demographics* 12 (February 1990): 30-33.

———. "Your Money or Your Time." *American Demographics* 13 (November 1991): 22-26.

Ryan, Michael. "How to Save Kids from TV." *Parade Magazine,* June 21, 1992, p. 10.

St. Peters, Michelle, et al. "Television and Families: What Do Young Children Watch with Their Parents?" *Child Development* 62 (December 1991): 1409-23.

Salomon, Gavriel. "Cognitive Effects with and of Computer Technology." *Communication Research* 17 (February 1990): 26-44.

Sang, Fritz, et al. "Individuation and Television Coviewing in the Family:

Developmental Trends in the Viewing Behavior of Adolescents." *Journal of Broadcasting & Electronic Media* 36 (Fall 1992): 427-41.

Schor, Juliet. *The Overworked American: The Unexpected Decline of Leisure.* New York: BasicBooks, 1991.

Schultze, Quentin J., et al. *Dancing in the Dark: Youth, Popular Culture and the Electronic Media.* Grand Rapids, Mich.: Eerdmans, 1991.

Singer, Dorothy G. *The Parent's Guide: Use TV to Your Child's Advantage.* Reston, Va.: Acropolis Books, 1990.

Smith, Thomas E. "Time and Academic Achievement." *Journal of Youth and Adolescence* 19, no. 6 (1990): 539-58.

Smykla, Margaret L. "Hope and Glory" [watching video movies with son]. *Film Comment* 28 (March/April 1992): 78.

Snarey, John. *How Fathers Care for the Next Generation: A Four-Decade Study.* Cambridge, Mass.: Harvard University Press, 1993.

Steinberg, Lawrence D. *You and Your Adolescent: A Parent's Guide for Ages 10 to 20.* New York: Harper & Row, 1990.

Taffel, Ron. "Making Your Child Feel Safe in a Scary World." *McCall's,* February 1993, pp. 60, 62-63.

Takanishi, Ruby. "Changing Views of Adolescence in Contemporary Society." *Teachers College Record* 94 (Spring 1993): 459-65.

Timmer, S. G., et al. "How Children Use Time." In *Time, Goods and Well-Being,* ed. F. T. Juster and F. B. Stafford (Ann Arbor: University of Michigan/Institute for Social Research, 1985).

Tobenkin, David. "Customers Respond to Video on Demand." *Broadcasting & Cable,* November 29, 1993, p. 16.

Trelease, Jim. *The New Read-Aloud Handbook.* New York: Penguin, 1989.

U.S. Department of Education, Office of Educational Research and Improvement. *National Assessment of Educational Progress, 1992 Reading Report Card for the Nation and the States.* Washington, D.C.: Government Printing Office, 1993.

Waldman, Steven, and Karen Springen. "Too Old Too Fast?" *Newsweek,* November 16, 1992, pp. 80-88.

Weaver, Barry, and Nancy Barbour. "Mediation of Children's Televiewing." *Families in Society* 73 (April 1992): 236-42.

Wernick, Sarah. "Video-Game Mania." *Working Mother,* June 1993, pp. 62-65.

Wilson, Barbara J., and Audrey J. Weiss. "Developmental Differences in Children's Reactions to a Toy Advertisement Linked to a Toy-Based Cartoon." *Journal of Broadcasting & Electronic Media* 36 (Fall 1992): 371-94.

Wood, Leonard. "Teenagers' Reading Habits." *Publishers Weekly,* July 29, 1988, p. 132.

"Would You Give Up TV for a Million Bucks?" *TV Guide,* October 10-16, 1992, pp. 10-13.

Additional Resources

Arp, Claudio, and Linda Dillow. *The Big Book of Family Fun*. Nashville: Thomas Nelson, 1994.

Bennett, Steve, and Ruth Bennett. *365 TV-Free Activities You Can Do with Your Child*. Holbrook, Mass.: Bob Adams, 1991.

Bertolini, Rebecca. *Mom's Big Activity Book*. Wheaton, Ill.: Victor Books, 1992.

Brown, Nadine M. *How to Have Kids with Character*. Wheaton, Ill.: Tyndale House, 1990.

Erickson, Donna. *Prime Time Together with Kids*. Minneapolis: Augsburg, 1989.

Faber, Adele, and Elaine Mazlish. *How to Talk So Kids Will Listen and Listen So Kids Will Talk*. New York: Avon Books, 1980.

Gaither, Gloria, and Shirley Dobson. *Let's Make a Memory: Great Ideas for Building Family Traditions and Togetherness*. Dallas: Word, 1983.

Gore, Tipper. *Raising PG Kids in an X-Rated Society*. New York: Bantam, 1987.

Greene, Lawrence J. *1001 Ways to Improve Your Child's Schoolwork*. New York: Dell, 1991.

Hamilton, Leslie. *Child's Play 6-12: 160 Instant Activities, Crafts and Science Projects for Grade Schoolers*. New York: Crown, 1991.

Hedrick, Lucy H. *365 Ways to Save Time with Kids*. New York: Hearst Books, 1993.

Horie, Michiaki, and Hildegard Horie. *Whatever Became of Fathering?* Downers Grove, Ill.: InterVarsity Press, 1993.

Johnson, Spencer. *The One Minute Father*. New York: Morrow, 1983.

Kaye, Peggy. *Games for Learning*. New York: Noonday, 1991.

McManus, Michael J. *50 Practical Ways to Take Our Kids Back from the World*. Wheaton, Ill.: Tyndale House, 1993.

Patterson, Richard, Jr. *It's the Little Things That Count*. Nashville: Thomas Nelson, 1993.

Peel, Kathy, and Judie Byrd. *A Mother's Manual for Holiday Survival*. Colorado Springs, Colo.: Focus on the Family, 1991.

Peel, Kathy, and Joy Mahaffy. *A Mother's Manual for Schoolday Survival*. Colorado Springs, Colo.: Focus on the Family, 1990.

Phillips, Phil. *52 Things for Your Kids to Do Instead of Watching TV*. Nashville: Thomas Nelson, 1992.

Thigpen, Paul, and Leisa Thigpen. *52 Simple Ways to Build Family Traditions*. Nashville: Thomas Nelson, 1994.

Tuttle, Cheryl, and Penny Paquette. *Thinking Games to Play with Your Child*. Los Angeles: Lowell House, 1991.

Van Klompenburg, Carol, and Joyce K. Ellis. *When the Kids Are Home from School*. Minneapolis: Bethany House, 1991.

Readers may contact the author by writing or calling:

Quentin J. Schultze
Communication Arts & Sciences Department
Calvin College
3201 Burton S.E.
Grand Rapids, MI 49546
(616) 957-6290
Internet: schu@calvin.edu

Winning Your Kids Back from the Media is also available in a video curriculum kit, including a video, book and study guide. For information, contact:

Gospel Films and Video
P.O. Box 455
Muskegon, MI 49443
1-800-253-0413